WESTMAR COLLEGE LIBRARY

W9-BWU-415

S. R.

EPUBLIC

MONGOLIA

Great
Wall   Ming Tombs

PEKING

N   A

Huang

Yangtze

Nanking

Hangchow

Canton

Hong Kong

South

China Sea

KOREA

JAPAN

Sea

of Japan

Yellow

Sea

Shanghai

East

China

Sea

TAIWAN

CHINA

0   100   500

A China Passage

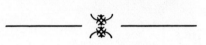

Also by John Kenneth Galbraith

American Capitalism:
The Concept of Countervailing Power

A Theory of Price Control

Economics and the Art of Controversy

The Great Crash 1929

The Affluent Society

The Liberal Hour

The Scotch

The New Industrial State

The Triumph

Indian Painting
(*with Mohinder Singh Randhawa*)

Ambassador's Journal

Economics, Peace and Laughter

A China Passage

John Kenneth Galbraith

ILLUSTRATED WITH
PHOTOGRAPHS
BY MARC RIBOUD
AND
ENDPAPER MAP
BY SAMUEL H. BRYANT

BOSTON
HOUGHTON MIFFLIN COMPANY
1973

915.1
G148
DS
711
.G32

FIRST PRINTING C

Copyright © 1973 by John Kenneth Galbraith
Photographs copyright © Marc Riboud/Magnum
All rights reserved. No part of this work may
be reproduced or transmitted in any form by any means,
electronic or mechanical, including photocopying and
recording, or by any information storage or retrieval
system, without permission in writing
from the publisher.

ISBN: 0-395-16615-2
LIBRARY OF CONGRESS CATALOG CARD NUMBER: 72-11340
PRINTED IN THE UNITED STATES OF AMERICA

Selections from this book have appeared in
Progressive magazine and *The New York Times Magazine*

87098

for Emily Wilson with love

"As for the imperialist countries, we should unite with their peoples and strive to coexist peacefully with those countries, do business with them and prevent any possible war, but under no circumstances should we harbor any unrealistic notions about them."

— MAO TSE-TUNG

Foreword

The justification for this book is simple, almost distress-ingly so. I had a chance to go to China and most people do not. It occurred to me, as I mention in the early pages, that I might tell everything that one sees, hears, thinks, remembers on such a visit from the moment he leaves un-til he is home again. That I tried to do. I'm not quite sure it is all here. But surely all will agree that for so short a trip, it is not so short a book.

I emphasize that this is a visitor's view of China. I am not a Chinese expert. I am not especially well read on Chinese history or economics. Our trip was arranged to give us a privileged view of the Chinese economic system; even here I imagine we learned much that shrewd ob-servers have already known.* But since returning every-

* "The big generalizations are all agreed upon: There has been a tre-mendous betterment of the material life and morale of the common people. Incredible hard work has produced a credible miracle reshaping both land and people . . . But China is not America. Individualism is not esteemed. Art and letters are at a mass propaganda level. The national political process remains shrouded in mystery. Higher education is slowly reviving after a four-year shutdown." John K. Fairbank, "To China and Back," *The New York Review of Books*, October 19, 1972.

one I've encountered has asked: What's it really like? This, as it seemed each day, is what it is really like.

The avowed purpose of our journey was to obtain a picture of the Chinese economy. This is not something that can be made to emerge from day-to-day reactions to industrial establishments, markets, communes or discussions with economists and officials. One must sit down and try to put it all together. This I did in Paris on my way home, and it comes into the book as a long day's thoughts toward the end. There is a little repetition here which I could not avoid for I had to draw on some earlier observations.

Many, many years ago at Time, Inc., there were two classes of people — those who worked for *Life* and those of us who believed that one word was worth a thousand pictures. The last is still my faith. But there are exceptions to all rules. Briefly in Peking, during my visit, was Marc Riboud, the great French photographer whose photographs of China I had earlier seen and extravagantly admired. He offered to let me have some pictures of the wonders I here describe. I am deeply grateful.

I have other important debts to acknowledge. The first is to our Chinese hosts, especially to the members of the Chinese Academy of Sciences, the Chinese Scientific and Technical Association and the members of the faculty of the University of Peking. A second is to the Federation of American Scientists and its Executive Director, Dr. Jeremy Stone, who arranged our visit. And I am greatly indebted to my two colleagues, Professor James Tobin of Yale and Professor Wassily Leontief of Harvard, both my seniors in office as President of the American Economic Association. I happily free them from any responsibility of any kind for anything I have here written. But I cannot be prevented from saying that they were the most wise and agreeable of companions. And I am much in their debt for the questions they asked and the discussion they invited and from which I benefited.

A China Passage

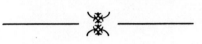

September 4, Labor Day—Out of Boston

I'm on my way to China — the most successful of five recent attempts — and I should be grateful to Richard Nixon. Instead, within reasonable limits, I propose to write down everything I hear or think and describe everything I see or seem to see.

My first China effort, omitting an earlier passage which I might later mention, was four years ago and involved the Rumanians. They promised through Georges-Henri Martin, the highly competent editor of *La Tribune de Genève,* to see if they could arrange it. Ted Kennedy was to go; I was promoter and hitchhiker. I made a trip to Bucharest to negotiate arrangements following some devious meetings in Geneva. The plane I was to take from Zurich to Bucharest was Flight 215 of the Rumanian airline leaving at 1:10 P.M. I carefully noted this as Flight 110 leaving at 2:15 P.M. and sat in the Zurich airport watching the plane and wondering why they were pulling it away from the ramp. It was depressing to see it take off. I got to Bucharest a day late; the Rumanians were understanding. My negotiations went well but to make final plans it was necessary that they include Kennedy. The further meeting was to be in Paris. But it was never possible to get Kennedy there for the rendezvous. There was always a vote in the Senate.

Later the Swiss Ambassador in Peking was asked if he would ask for me. It was, in a way, a payoff. I had delivered a lecture at the University of Geneva while some striking students were occupying the Rector's office. Halfway through my lecture they called off the strike — and came to the lecture. It seems possible they lacked dedication. After a luncheon later in Bern a member of the Swiss Federal Council thanked me for my competent strike-breaking. I responded by asking for intercession in Peking. The Swiss Ambassador sent back word that the time was not ripe.

Still later I had lunch one day at Hotel zum Storchen in Zurich with Han Suyin, the novelist. She was on her way to the Middle Kingdom where, rightly, she is well regarded. She asked someone for me and got word that I was persona non grata. I had once advocated a Two-China Policy. That is true. I had long urged that the door be open to Peking when this was the extreme of radicalism, and, in fact, it caused me a bad morning with the Senate Foreign Relations Committee when I wanted very much to be confirmed as Ambassador to India. Frank Lausche, then Senator from Ohio, a man who knew, off-hand, the location of both China and India, was quite mean in his reaction.

My fourth effort was three years ago. It is a revealing

story on how favors are done, influence is used. During my years in India I saw much of Zulfikar Ali Bhutto who was then Pakistan's Foreign Minister. We had both been at Berkeley, he rather more recently than I. We talked fruitlessly and at terrible length but amiably about Kashmir. In 1969, now out of office, he wrote me that his daughter, brilliant, mature, handsome, had been denied admission to Radcliffe because of her age. She was only sixteen. He asked me to intercede. I did so, aware that not God, not Jesus, not even nuclear fission, could move a Radcliffe Dean of Admissions. I learned that the earlier decision had already been reversed. Pinkie Bhutto, as she has since come to be known with much affection in our family, was in. I conveyed the news to her father and did not dwell excessively on the timing of my plea in relation to result. He thanked me and said, "if there is ever anything I can do for you . . ." I knew he was on warm terms with the Chinese; I mentioned my yearning. He tried and got word back that the Chinese were troubled by the growing intimacy between the U.S. and the U.S.S.R. Visits of "notable personalities" from the United States would, it was felt, somehow give blessing to this liaison, or so I was told.

Now I am going. The Federation of American Scientists, an excellent organization of mainly liberal scientists, has been arranging exchanges. The moving and energetic spirit is Jeremy Stone, the son of my old friend I. F. (Izzy) Stone of the famous newsletter. I am the nominal leader of a delegation consisting of myself and my two predecessors as President of the American Economic Association —

Wassily Leontief of Harvard and James Tobin of Yale. The American Economic Association (AEA to its members) is the professional organization of economists and more liberal on the whole than the AMA or even the ABA. One is elected by a form of democratic centralism that would make Lenin blush. You are nominated by the established scholars and run on a ballot with a blank space into which any other name could be written, yours being printed. Bernie Cornfeld might not lose. My duties are nominal, my honors fleeting. Nothing should more induce a contrite heart. But being President of the American Economic Association now seems a great thing. It gets me to China.

One leaves for China by spending a week doing what was postponed all summer — letters, a foreword to Eric Hodgins's posthumous and totally joyous memoirs, reading three other manuscripts including a novel that I do not understand, writing a last-minute review of George Kennan. Hasty treatment for George. Then at high and golden noon today I took leave of our grandson, our burnished Vermont meadows, our beavers and lake and the marvelous great waste of land that we bought for something less than five dollars an acre in the year 1947.

In Boston at the airport the agent saw that my destination was Hong Kong and said, "Quite a trip." I said firmly, "Peking, in fact." He said, "Do you need a special visa or anything?" Then I took leave of my wife, the world's most passionate traveler. The Federation of American Scientists had absolutely forbidden wives. She was distraught — but at not going, not at losing me. I was sad to leave her behind, but would have felt worse had she been going instead of me. Because of hijacking, every bag was being checked, everyone was being electronically frisked. I was waved through; they knew I was going somewhere important. My bag was full of presents, all nonmetallic.

What does one take to China? Not ball points or lipsticks or other artifacts of a consumer culture. These are surely derogatory. I settled with the help of Mrs. Andrea Williams (my ally against the world, my authority in all matters of taste) on several copies of Edgar Snow's *Red Star over China*, some books on Wyeth, another on Chinese bronzes and a truly magnificent sample of my own works.

Mention of Mrs. Williams reminds me of the problem of protocol that arose to imperil this journey. The Chinese advised me through Jeremy Stone that our visas would be issued in Ottawa. Mrs. Williams sent up the passports. The Chinese Embassy called back. "So sorry." My passport said, ". . . not valid for travel to, in or through Communist controlled portions [sic] of . . . China." Could a visa go with such a passport? Well, hardly. The prohibition had been lifted but the offending words remained. We consulted the State Department — surely a little help for a former ambassador . . . ? Someone suggested that a man from our Embassy in Ottawa might go to the Chinese Embassy and remove the restriction. Anyone could. The words were obsolete. Our Embassy considered and concluded that, since China is not recognized, no officer of theirs could go inside the doors of the Chinese Embassy. A more direct approach commended itself. Hazel Denton,

5

my erstwhile assistant and perpetual friend, has a brother, not long ago retired from the Royal Air Force, who works in Ottawa for Honeywell. He has a German wife, a woman of style and presence. She walked into the Chinese Embassy, asked for my passport, received it and struck out the offending restriction with black India ink. The visa came forth promptly.

I am en route to China but, as the next installment will tell, the still pallid prospects of George McGovern will interpose their claims.

September 5 — Out of San Francisco

This was to be a full record of a trip to China. Accordingly let me advise that I had an astonishingly good dinner on TWA, saw Charlie Chaplin in *Modern Times*, the first movie I've ever completely endured on an airplane with the exception of *The Lavender Hill Mob*, and arrived in San Francisco at 8:30 P.M., more or less on time. There I had dinner (again) with Phyllis McCusker, who once lived in our house, became my secretary and now studies Italian at Berkeley. Berkeley she finds conventional and unexciting. Things might however become more interesting: there is a rumor that Ronald Reagan's economies might force the University to abolish the Italian Department.

This morning, according to schedule, I got up at 6:30 A.M. to await transportation by the McGovern organization to numerous television stations. The man who was to collect me overslept and — since someone had thoughtfully included the address of the first station — I went by myself. Donald Rumsfeld, the head of Nixon's Cost of Living Council, preceded me on the air. He blamed all of the economic difficulties of the Nixon Administration on mismanagement inherited from Lyndon Johnson: the Vietnam costs had been piled on expanded welfare programs with terrible results. When my turn came, I pointed out that were McGovern elected, according to Rumsfeld's argument, he wouldn't be responsible for anything bad until his second term. While I was making this compelling point, my trainer arrived, apologetic. That was ABC, then came a news show, radio and NBC. All wanted to know most whether I had enjoyed debating Buckley at the two conventions in Miami. I said I did, which is so. Bill Buckley is the ideal opponent — pleasant, quick in response, invulnerable to insult and invariably wrong.

The questions on the campaign had to do with McGovern's economics and included matters on which he has not yet taken a position. My method was to identify him firmly with what is right. That is where a good man will end up anyway; you should do as well for your candidate as possible. George was in town yesterday and was well received. I have difficulty believing he can make it, and I equally doubt that he is as far behind as the polls show. Nixon's handicap, personality apart, is not the Watergate scandal but the rich, particularly the John Connally Democrats. Theirs is the Benedict Arnold effect made worse by the fact that they are self-righteous, selfish and very much against paying proper taxes. My description of them as a bunch of dropouts from the Federal tax system evoked applause even from the camera crews.

I was asked in the last show for a thumbnail sketch of my career in politics. I had to say that it has all been downhill. Slightly in 1940 and in volume in 1952 and 1956, I wrote speeches. That meant being at the very center of the action. Newspapermen, especially in 1952 and 1956, treated me with courtesy and respect. The local politicians sought me out in the hope that I would put a few words in their praise or a few gems of their wisdom in the next draft. Once Eric Sevareid stopped me in an airport and said with terrible intelligence, "Adlai needs to make a great speech. It's his only chance."

By 1960 things had changed for the worse. I was sent out to make speeches myself. My specialty was precincts so benightedly anti-Catholic that the only question in the local mind was whether Kennedy would telephone the Pope before or after each meeting of the National Security Council. But someone had to go. You cannot ignore enthusiastic and egregiously optimistic supporters. In that campaign I was buoyed up by the applause of some of the most hopeless minorities in the history of democratic government.

By 1968 and Gene McCarthy there was not even oratory. I was asked only to raise money. The war, an appeal to reason, then the hard sell. By the Convention I could guess within a hundred dollars what an audience would yield. My future in politics is now entirely asking for money. A glum prospect.

With many others I believe San Francisco to be, next to London, the most agreeable large city in the world. Unlike others I know the reason. The location explains something. The hills, like narrow streets, keep cars from moving at a nerve-rending speed as they do in Paris or sometimes on Fifth Avenue. But the yet more important reason is that hotel desks, hotel rooms, airport counters, drugstores, restaurants are extensively manned by polite and friendly Orientals rather than surly Anglo-Saxons. The Fairmont Hotel is agreeable; this is partly the big wine-red rug, partly because even the crevices are clean. But mostly it's the nicer staff.

I made the plane comfortably at one in the afternoon — Pan Am. The food was bad but in an uninspired way. Except for the shrimp no real thought had been given to making it awful. The shrimp had been soaked in synthetic rubber. Each one was good for an hour's chewing. The passengers' service agent in San Francisco used to be in Hong Kong; he remembered me favorably from ten years ago. Poor fellow, he got promoted and has never ceased to mourn the sights and smells of the China coast — so he told me. I hope he doesn't have to eat the Pan Am food too.

September 6 — Out of Honolulu

I was welcomed last night by the local and eclectic McGovern organization — one Chinese, one Japanese, one unidentified and one over twenty. They took me to a

McGovern-oriented gas station where all the profits go to the campaign. This is something new and possibly damaging to the candidate's stand on percentage depletion. For the television cameras I filled a couple of cars and tanked up the one that was carrying me. Even at my primitive level, politics forces one to do completely unnatural things. I could not handle a gasoline hose with the slightest plausibility.

After the gas station I swam blissfully for an hour off Waikiki, slept even more blissfully for an hour and then addressed a sizable gathering of psychologists (meeting in convention) on the merits of McGovern, of which they were already fully persuaded, and his need for money, on which they may have been less clear. I also gave various press interviews, had a sandwich and staggered into bed.

This morning I swam again in the glittering early sunlight before breakfast. The beach was all mine; overnight, some excellent machine had sifted out the cigarette butts, the empty sun tan tubes, the used condoms and the other detritus of an advanced civilization. Captain Cook, looking at the clean sand, would have felt at home. The forest of high-rises would have puzzled him. After breakfast I did nothing until taken to the airport for another television and press session. The Hawaiian preoccupation, judging from the questions, is not with abortion, marijuana, welfare reform or other great subjects. It is exclusively with the effect of McGovern's defense cuts — do they portend another disaster at Pearl Harbor? I answered that no one would wish to continue defense spending in order to provide employment. Some lie, that. Then

I argued that McGovern, having proposed the cuts, had been forced to consider the public service employment, the severance pay, the other (unspecified) reconversion measures that would ease the transition. Nixon, on the other hand, had already gone in for unplanned, helter-skelter cuts from which people, as in Seattle, had really suffered. Finally I noted that Hawaii did not manufacture ABMs and space shuttles and that the Navy and Air Force would probably survive. Senator Eagleton, when here, was probably more honest. He said it would be bad, and people should be braced for the worst.

We were frisked with exceptional thoroughness before boarding. Natacha Stewart, of *The New Yorker* short stories (and *Evil Eye*), was once given an especially competent going-over by a woman in Zurich. The Swiss are meticulous on this matter. When it was over, she asked the woman if she enjoyed her work.

Let me now explain that this is my second trip to China. In autumn 1945, with Paul Nitze, later Deputy Defense Secretary, Paul Baran, the famous Marxist economist, and others I was in Tokyo with the United States Strategic Bombing Survey. Our military adviser was the late Major General Orvil Anderson, who had been operations head of the Eighth Air Force in Europe and whose military career was later to end when he publicly proposed bombing the Soviet nuclear establishments as a contribution to a more durable peace. President Truman fired him. There were extenuating circumstances but Truman did not know. Orvil was the world's champion nonstop talker. In the natural course of events he was bound to have proposed everything; otherwise he would have run out of material.

During the twenties, as a close friend of Brigadier General William (Billy) Mitchell, Orvil had conceived a deep, unremitting and rather imaginative hatred for Douglas MacArthur who had been a judge when Mitchell was court-martialed. MacArthur may have had more going for him than was realized at the time. The precedent of court-martialing air generals was one that he was right to help set and in the national interest. It had hurt Orvil to be always reading in Europe of the great distances that MacArthur had to traverse in the Pacific. He proposed to prove to us, using the unbelievable excuse that we were inspecting bases, that you could go the whole way (though in reverse) in one day. We started out late one evening from Tokyo in Orvil's, i.e., the U.S. Government's, B–17, flew around Mount Fuji in full moonlight — a great glittering cone that still shines in the eye of my mind — and then, for some reason, diverted ourselves to Shanghai where we arrived an hour or two after dawn. It was foggy when we came overhead and, while waiting, we did a short air tour up the Yangtze toward Nanking. Something had to be done to the airplane so Paul Nitze and I went into town. As we were waiting for our transport, a GI in handcuffs was being hustled aboard a MATS (Military Air Transport Service) plane. Paul asked the sergeant what he had done. The sergeant replied, "Well, goin' through security just now, we found haffa million American dollars on him. We don't think he got it honest."

He had got the money, without doubt, as a crew member of one of the planes flying between Chungking, Peking and Shanghai. In each city, depending on the local supply of money and goods, there was a different rate of exchange between the Chinese yuan and the American dollar. Though untutored in economics our soldiers had grasped the subtle idea of arbitrage — buying U.S. dollars dear and selling them even dearer — with astonishing speed.

Shanghai — in contrast with Tokyo which was then a vast burned-over waste — seemed a city of unbelievable opulence. The shops were filled with every kind of merchandise — silks and brocades were in special abundance. Paul and I had an overpowering urge to go shopping. An exceptionally solvent member of the Establishment — his identification is with the Pratt family which sold out late and high to Rockefeller and Standard Oil — Paul was totally without funds. He tried to cash a check at the newly reopened National City Bank. He was treated with contempt — a palpable paperhanger. We shared some $50, which I had.

That night we flew on to Manila, and a civilian accountant for some United States firm with Pacific interests (then being rehabilitated) hitched a ride. No two-star general with an airplane had ever talked to him before. Paul and I had long since learned to take evasive action when Orvil attacked. Our passenger was innocent and willing. Through the long night Orvil lectured him on the history of manned flight since Icarus. From that, he went on to his favorite subject of conversation — a brief mention each of the several hundred missions flown by the Eighth Air Force followed by a detailed commentary on the tactical and strategic theory lying back of each.[1] The engines of a B-17 are (or were) close inboard, and there is (or was) no insulation. Orvil's competition was great, even if also repetitious. By morning he had completely lost his voice. The rest of the trip was utterly serene. We requisitioned a C-47 and did a close inspection of Corregidor and Bataan. By then subtropical growth had erased almost every trace of the war. Before World War II, in addition to the guns of Corregidor, a concrete island in the shape of a battleship protected the approaches to Manila Bay. A general outlined a new defense concept — not a concrete battleship but a concrete aircraft carrier. Paul and I endorsed this static aberration of the military mind. Orvil could only croak his dissent.

Next morning, loaded with gasoline including the extra

[1] He had been operations head of the Eighth Air Force, the bomber force which operated against the Continent from England. Reminiscence easily gets out of hand; Ramsey Potts, a very young and most remarkable colonel on his staff, once recalled how Orvil got the job. It tells something of the USAAF in its salad days. Orvil was in Washington on a headquarters assignment. A man of tactless, as well as enduring, speech, he one day infuriated General Henry (Hap) Arnold, the head of the Air Force. Arnold said, "General, would you go to Bolling Field this afternoon and get aboard whatever airplane is going the greatest distance from Washington?" Orvil asked, "Is that an order?" Arnold said, "I've never given one with more feeling in my life."

An airplane was going to England. Orvil got aboard and went out to High Wycombe, the command post of the Eighth. There he had nothing to do but talk. But one afternoon the bombers went out, and General Doolittle, the commander, went into London to have a uniform fitted. Presently the weather people arrived in a panic. All of southern England was about to close in. A total English fog. Not long before, the same thing had happened to RAF Bomber Command when it was out. The hills and hedgerows of England were littered with the remnants of Lancasters and Wellingtons and their occupants. There was no one at High Wycombe with the authority to recall the planes. Orvil stepped in and did. No one thereafter could refuse him a job.

tanks in the bomb bay, we took off before dawn to prove
that the MacArthur odyssey could easily be accomplished
in a day. And we flew all day — down the Philippine
archipelago, on to the ocean beyond, on to Morotai which
we circled, on and on, on to the coast of New Guinea, on
to Hollandia, on to Manus in the Admiralties. We whiled
away the day playing poker in the waist of the bomber.
Orvil was still silent. At nine that night we landed at
Manus — still a long way short of the MacArthur starting
point at Guadalcanal. The distance was greater than I
had ever imagined. It seemed to me incredible that it
took only three years. Next morning when the plane was
refueled, it was learned that the gas gauges were defective.
We had landed with less than fifteen minutes' fuel in the
tanks. The slightest circling in the dark and the engines
would have started to sputter. Orvil recovered his voice
to take the matter up with the pilot. I was glad.

September 8 — At the Border

A day has been lost because of the date line. No more
reminiscence; the present must be faced. We are in China.
I met Leontief in Tokyo airport yesterday evening; we
arrived in Hong Kong at ten last night. Tobin came in
this morning from Nairobi where he is teaching this year.
At 10:30 A.M., the China Travel Service, which inhabits
a busy office behind the Peninsula Hotel, dispatched us
by train across the New Territories. A guide came along

15

to keep us from getting nervous. It's an hour to the border over untidy and, oddly enough, often unpopulated countryside. There is something wrong with the scale of the maps showing Hong Kong; on these it's no distance at all. At intervals are rice paddies and vegetable gardens of great opulence. At a station just short of the border all passengers not going to China were disembarked. Not many continued.

The border, as many must have told, is unprepossessing — very understated by, say, Berlin standards. There are towers on the hills, some smattering, I thought, of a local fence and a tiny bridge. The train stops on one side of the bridge. We showed papers for departure from Hong Kong but entered China with almost no formality. After we walked across the bridge, our passports were collected but we were told, with just a trace of emphasis, that our baggage was exempt from any scrutiny. There was a considerable bustle of people passing back toward Hong Kong. Our only immediately visible companion going the other way was a handsome dark man from Nigeria on the way to organize a Ping-Pong match. Mr. Wong of the Kwangtung branch of the Chinese Scientific and Technical Association (one of our hosts) materialized we had our picture taken before a vast and benign statue of Chairman Mao, and the real business of our trip began with a simple but superb lunch served in the station dining room. Now we are waiting for the train for Canton. My writing is not helped by a loudspeaker which belches decibels of infinite strength from somewhere in the ceiling over my head. It has just changed to a song with a certain martial strain. We learn that it is the victory march of the Democratic Republic of Vietnam. Judging by the results over the years it must be a very good song.

Later in Canton

The train from the border to Canton is fast, air-conditioned, with lace-curtained windows and a cosmopolitan passenger list which today included a Counsellor at the Canadian Embassy with his beautiful Japanese wife, three gentlemen of Indian extraction from Mauritius on their way to Peking (also to arrange athletic affairs) and a professor and his wife from Sri Lanka (née Ceylon), formerly of Toronto, Ontario. They are not arranging anything, merely curious. All stopped by for a chat.

The countryside is gorgeous — rich green rice fields, sugar cane, a little hemp, vegetables and bamboo, neat like a big garden. It is an enchanting prospect, not different from Bengal except for the distant, misty hills.

We were welcomed at the Canton station with much warmth and considerable ceremony by (among others) representatives of the Chinese Scientific and Technical Association and brought to bright, comfortable rooms high in the rather cavernous East Hotel. Our itinerary, so far a complete mystery, was partly revealed to us; we go to Peking tomorrow afternoon. After an hour for sleep we toured the city, ending with a rooftop view of the whole from a high building by the river.

Nothing could have departed more from my preconception. The older streets are arcaded like those of Calcutta but are wide and straight and — by New York standards — of cleanly elegance. The latter comes from having been washed and swept in the recent past. The river flows with traffic; most of it, we were told, was country boats from the communes returning after delivering their produce. Some have engines, more depend on manpower. On the fast-flowing stream it is all very exciting. Once large numbers lived on boats. The typhoons greatly reduced life expectancy. Now, we were told, the people are mostly housed on solid land and are quite safe.

The bicycle population rivals that of New Delhi now or of Copenhagen forty years ago — a great, endless, rolling tide. One studies the faces; everyone seems to be in excellent humor. No solemn social conclusions are justified. Cyclists do not expect traffic jams; one can easily evade the man ahead. Motorists must be alert for trouble, expect the worst in traffic or insult. So they look tense, angry or resigned. On the streets here there are no cars, our official vehicles apart. But there are lots of trucks, and we and they make up for our lack of numbers with continuous horn-blowing so one is not totally oppressed by the calm.

Before the revolution — liberation is the approved term — Canton was a trading center; some of the big houses of the compradors, rich in stonework, survive along the river. Now the city makes textiles, machinery, bicycles, chemical fibers and has a promising amount of air pollution — the factory chimneys roll out a particularly dense particulate matter. I mentioned this and was told that the problem was receiving urgent attention. That formula makes one feel at home. I asked why people seemed to be work-

ing so hard and was told that it was because of Chairman
Mao and the feeling that the country now belongs to them.
I inquired also as to what happened if a factory did badly.
That has not yet happened. My colleagues were not
greatly more successful with their questions except when,
in accordance with established professional custom, we
answered each other's questions ourselves.

Much later in Canton

Our welcoming dinner was by the Principal Responsible
Person (which is modern Chinese for president or boss)
of the Scientific and Technical Association of Kwangtung
Province. Being hungry when the food arrived, I consumed plentifully. Full, I felt better. Alas, there was a
mistake; that food was not the dinner but only the first
of seven equally stunning courses. We were toasted prop-
erly with proposals for many happy returns. Conversation
turned on politics rather than economics — the advantage
of a prompt American exit from Vietnam and Taiwan.
(These subjects were scarcely again to be mentioned.)
We encouraged no argument. I did plead for patience on
the ground that it took the United States a long time to
change its mind even when wrong. This adds greatly to
the stability of our conduct in international affairs. Jim
Tobin mentioned as unfortunate the Chinese veto of Bangladesh's entry into the United Nations. Our hosts did
not defend the action. It may be that, this being a small
matter, the defense was not yet an available currency.
The interest in cultural and scientific exchange seemed
exceedingly real. Russia came up, and I hazarded the

thought that the United States should remain scrupulously apart from any quarrel between China and the social imperialists. This also evoked no comment. More sociably we were all asked the number of our children, their ages, state of their education if any, and the number who were sons.

September 9 — Canton, Peking

This morning was devoted to sightseeing and by no means to be deplored. But first a matter of nutrition. Last winter a ten-year-old friend of ours in Switzerland asked me to ask William Buckley on his return from China the one question on which he said there was no available information: What in China do you have for breakfast? The answer, at the East Hotel in Canton (the work of an architect whose great idea was a forthright waste of space), is first juice, then toast, coffee, bacon and eggs as you prefer. Service is accomplished by inordinately good-natured and obliging waiters, all in the basic white-shirt-blue-trouser-well-washed national costume. After breakfast we went first to the Pavilion Overlooking the Sea, sometimes called the Five Story Pagoda, a burgundy-red structure of great beauty which once kept watch over the Pearl River and town and is now dedicated to the history of Chinese ceramics. My knowledge of ceramics was improved by several hundred percent during the morning though it is still negligible. This is the result of a very low base. One fascinating modern creation shows on a large field the arrival of the revolution in a Chinese village. At one end a landlord of superbly arrogant mien, a bit on the scholarly side, is presiding pleasurably over the exploitation of his tenants. This he does from his chair; the actual work of exploitation is accomplished by an appalling collection of ruffians. Soon the revolution comes; there is a confusing battle; presently the landlord is appealing pitifully for mercy. One doubts that he was rehabilitated. At the end the people are triumphant and much better fed. I liked it. The late Ming pieces are less ambitious but more beautiful.

Then we went to the pagoda at the Temple of the Six Banyan Trees which towers over the city for nine stories (seventeen inside) and is everything a pagoda should be and hence needs no further description. From there we went on to the park which memorializes the first — unsuccessful — conflict of the Communists with the Kuomintang in 1927. The park is vast, with pavilions in the traditional style and quite a few quotations from Chairman Mao. It is a good park. Two huge curved-roof pavilions celebrate Korean and Sino-Soviet friendship. We turned first toward the Korean pavilion.

Next we crossed the Pearl River, dense with traffic at this time of day, to tour (at our request) the industrial quarter — all wholly basic industries, including a tool factory, a boiler factory and a badminton and Ping-Pong equipment factory. Interspersed were workers' flats, decent and clean if untidy and less than opulent. Everywhere the bicycle traffic filled the streets. Everywhere people looked washed and busy. I once estimated that you could cross the whole of Madras from the airport to the American Consulate and not see more than ten people in each hundred employed or moving in any visibly purposeful way. The rest were unemployed or anyhow not working. Here, children apart, the corresponding proportion of purposeful people is about 90 percent.

We lunched at the hotel. As we are determined to master Chinese table manners, we asked for chopsticks. Then we were served beef bouillon and lamb chops. Thereafter I slept for two hours, and we departed for the airport. Now we are halfway to Peking, and I will never make it. I have the middle seat on a five-abreast plane with leg room designed for Chinese. (It is a Soviet-built turboprop.) All feeling has gone from my legs. Amputation would no longer help — it would make no difference one way or the other and never be noticed.

Later

I penned the above in the dark before the dawn just before a light showed at the end of my tunnel. A steward tapped my shoulder, pointed to my paraplegic limbs and led me — supported me — back to a curtained-off couch at the back of the plane. There I slept for two hours while we made two landings — one very rough and dangerous, the plane careening madly between the Ming Tombs, then another better landing, after which I awoke to find we were, in fact, on the ground.

At Peking we were welcomed by members of the Revolutionary Committee and the Responsible Persons of the

Faculty of Economics at the University of Peking and the Academy of Sciences to the number of a dozen or so. The welcome, as at Canton, was warm; the speeches, including my own, on friendly cooperation between peoples were deficient in originality and content. But they are a long step on from the warnings of four or five years back about a billion Asian Communists debouching over Asia armed with nuclear weapons. Fairly high marks must be given to the men who moved us on this path, meaning Messrs. Nixon and Kissinger.

The first impression of Peking (by now at midnight) like that of Canton defeats all expectations — only more so. It is of incredible space. One comes in over hundred-yard-wide streets, empty except for occasional stray bicycles, and by the enormous Tien An Men Square fronting the Great Hall of the People and the Gate of Heavenly Peace leading to the Forbidden City. There was alarm over my 6 feet, 8½ inches at the Friendship Hotel — a number of multistory structures scattered over a small park in the western suburbs — and two beds were moved together. Thereafter we had a fine, friendly and informative dinner with the economists, of which more of the yield later. This time I correctly surmised that the first course was not the last. How wise! It is now well into the next day. Total, absolute silence pervades both hotel and city.

Our hosts propose that we spend the next two days on basic orientation — the Forbidden City, Ming Tombs, Great Wall, and then concentrate on how the country runs. This seems sensible. Much as I yearn to know

23

about economics, I yearn more to see the Forbidden City and the Wall. We learned at dinner, incidentally, that there is now a greatly increased concern in China for how the economies of other countries work. Japan, the United States and the Soviet Union were especially mentioned. We are expected to instruct as well as to learn. Nothing could be more suited to an economist's temperament.

Item: In Canton there were no keys to our hotel rooms. Jim Tobin left a plastic bag containing some new clothing on the train. He was assured — a hundred percent certain — that it would be found and returned. It was. A glass case by the dining room door of our Canton hotel contained lost and found items. Mostly combs. Years ago in Switzerland I noticed what a civilized convenience it is never to have to lock anything — even if the authorities sometimes disapprove. (A friend of mine there once had his car stolen — by an outpatient of a local insane asylum. The police recovered it and fined the owner ten francs for leaving the key in the ignition.) In China the respect for legal title seems even more complete. As with truth for conveying information, honesty acquired its excellent moral standing because at some distant time someone discovered that it was convenient and extraordinarily efficient. To the negative incentive of punishment in this world was then added the moral carrot of superior approval in the next.

Peking. In the distance
the Very Great Hall of the People

September 10 — Peking, the Friendship Hotel

The universities, as others have told, are still in turmoil following the Cultural Revolution. Students and able-bodied faculty, we learned last night, spend one third of their time in factories or People's Communes reassociating themselves with the masses. There is great emphasis on the need to identify theory with practice. Economics students, in particular, are expected to continue their study in the context of factory or farm. There seems also to be a fairly astringent attack on the parochial tendencies of academic departments. Our official host is not an economist; he is the head of the Revolutionary Committee at the University of Peking and a professor of Chinese.

All of this sounds rather grim but it also leads to disturbing lines of reflection. The recent American tendency in economics has been to divorce theory from any useful practice. We also rejoice in the cultivation of a student and faculty elite, hold it to be in the soundest tradition of democracy and are glad that, as economists, we are not mistaken for sociologists or professors of business administration. Rotating a few professors through General Motors, Young and Rubicam, Proctor and Gamble and ITT would be a wonderful corrective of the myths of the stalwart individual entrepreneur, the sovereign unmanaged consumer and a government superior to all economic interest — all these being thoughts which we now perpetuate. A spell in the factory might consolidate relations between student supporters of George McGovern and the minions of George Meany. On various occasions in the past I would gladly have exchanged the chairman of our department at Harvard for any available Chinese scholar. I conclude that we cannot get cultural exchange with the Chinese under way too rapidly.

This morning we passed back into the center of town observing the long lines awaiting admission to the First Asian Table Tennis Tournament. Our destination was the Forbidden City and, in particular, a display of recently unearthed antiquities in one of the pavilions. The catalogue title: "Antiquities Unearthed During the Great Proletarian Cultural Revolution." It was a stunning display — better, I thought, than the Tutankhamen show I saw last spring at the British Museum. And all are finds of the last half-dozen years. One can only imagine what remains to be dug up. There were marvelously decorated wine jugs, toys, tools, gold bowls, bronze and gilded lamps, an agate wine cup inlaid with gold, gold coins of the Chinese trade from Japan, Persia, Istanbul, an intricate Brueghel-like sculpture of acrobatic performers in glazed pottery of the Western Han Dynasty (206 B.C.–A.D. 8).

There was also a whole troop of bronze cavalry from the tomb of a general who felt the need for military protection in the next world. Yet another general, less concerned with tactical maneuver in the hereafter, had a squad of foot soldiers. There was a compelling reconstruction of the grave of a landlord, possibly a rather regressive character, who had himself buried in the company of eighteen of his slaves. The latter were buried alive which, from the landlord's point of view, would seem

27

logical for, if dead, they wouldn't be much help. The centerpiece of all was a burial garment (circa 113 B.C.) which was unearthed in Hopei in 1968 and which consists of 2498 pieces of jade held together with gold wire. The jade, a palish green, is in inch squares; the overall effect is that of a most elegant suit of armor complete with mask, boots and all. How practical it is could be another question. If there is any kind of a scramble on Judgment Day, it could be a bother.

Increasingly with advancing years I envy those who imagine a continuing and nonarthritic existence after death and are moved to take suitable precautions and make suitable arrangements. Both the thought and the activity must suppress unpleasant reflection.

This joyous excursion took all morning with time off for midmorning rest and tea. This afternoon, the Imperial Palaces.

Later

I had read about and seen pictures of the Forbidden City and the Imperial Palaces; my mind was prepared for large, mysterious, unkempt buildings scattered over an untidy, moated acreage. Unkempt it was once: we were told that hundreds of tons of refuse, including several inches of bird shit, were shoveled out in the post-liberation rehabilitation. It is still mysterious; the great roofs curve up to the sky, and the yellow, sometimes slightly greenish, tiles glisten in the sun. (Yellow tiles were reserved to the Emperor.) Lions of ferocious aspect guard the doors; dragons crawl over the stone walls, up marble ramps and,

Wonderful jade shroud though heavy
and maybe none too warm

naturally, up the backs of the dragon thrones. There are bronze tortoises of vast size and water birds of similar scale and composition which portend long life for those on the throne nearby. (Confidence in an afterlife was evidently not absolute.) But so far from being unkempt, everything is precise, beautiful and elegant.

The scale is also beyond belief. The gardens are miniature as compared with Versailles; but the palaces, in area, must be far more. When you have wandered through Versailles, you know where you have been; when you have seen a fraction of the Imperial Palaces, you do not know where you have been and both body and mind reject the effort to recall. We were guided from the Hall of Supreme Harmony to the Hall of Middle Harmony, to the Hall of Preserving Harmony, to the Palace of Heavenly Purity, to the Palace of Earthly Tranquility, to the Hall of Union, to the Hall of Royal Peace, to the Hall of Mental Cultivation, to the admirable Palace of Abstinence, to the quarters of various emperors, retired emperors (emperors did, on occasion, retire), empresses, sons, concubines, the latter mostly in the Palace of Blessings to Mother Earth, or, more appropriately, in the Palace of Gathering Excellence. En route or elsewhere we saw wonderful things in the most tremendous profusion: vases, jade carvings from tiny to tons in weight, other jewels, great gold vessels running to hundreds of kilograms, and finally the Imperial Garden replete with pines, cypresses and rocks, looking away to pagodas among the trees of a nearby hill.

After three hours I was in a trance — half weariness, half intoxication — and collapsed into our big, black-curtained limousine. I managed a little sleep before a long dinner with the faculty of the University of Peking. The latter involved a genuinely touching welcome from two Harvard economics Ph.D.'s, one of my generation, one much earlier, who had studied both at Harvard and with Professor John R. Commons of the University of Wisconsin. The dinner, at an old Chinese restaurant, was, perhaps, the most exquisite I ever consumed. It consisted of absolutely nothing but duck — duck hearts, duck liver, duck tail, duck wings, brown crisp duck skin, duck fuselage, duck soup from the bones. Voltaire said he would not be pecked to death by ducks. For these ducks he should have made an exception.

There was much expression of friendship and good will from the Vice Chairman of the Revolutionary Committee of the University of Peking, all of it warm and emphatic. I responded as best I could in kind.

Let me return to one of my Harvard friends. Now a Vice Chairman of the Revolutionary Committee of the Department of Economics, he did his work at Harvard under Charles J. Bullock. Bullock was a fascinating preparation for a career under Communism for he was the most famous reactionary of his time. His course in the History of Economic Thought ("from Adam to Adam Smith"), which I audited in 1934, was a legend for its bitter attacks on Herbert Hoover. Bullock considered Hoover an irresponsible radical. Roosevelt was President by then. But to Bullock he was simply unspeakable so he did not speak of him. John R. Commons, under whom my friend also worked, was more plausible. He was a progressive, thought by many a radical, and was the great academic ally of the elder La Follette.

31

Forbidden City: Vast. Elegant. Mysterious. Mystifying. Exhausting

September 11 — Peking

Historians are already agreed that one of Richard Nixon's more thoughtful and eloquent communiqués came after visiting the Great Wall: Roughly, "This is a Great Wall and only a great people with a great past could have a great wall and such a great people with such a great wall will surely have a great future." He might not have been so transcendent today. After a lovely trip northeast from Peking — corn, grain sorghum, cotton, vegetables and a general aspect of agricultural opulence — we ascended into the hills, and a combination of fog and drizzle closed in upon us. We could see only a few hundred yards of the Wall each way; the embankment carrying the MBTA is almost as impressive out toward Mattapan. It was better when we went for a walk on the top. This we did for some distance through several towers but not far enough to come to the first brick (the battlements are of long, darkish bricks) on which no name was scratched. The urge for such immortality employs all known alphabets; some recent Albanian visitors have distinguished themselves by adding country and date, all with a chisel that they evidently brought along for the work. Neither Nixon nor Kissinger is there, which is greatly to their credit. We did not look for Walter Cronkite.

After a nice lunch, brought along by our University of Peking hosts — cold roast chicken, hard-boiled eggs, apples, bread, cupcakes, beer and similar Chinese delicacies — we went out of the rest house to discover that the fog had partly lifted. There was the Wall, draping itself up one hill, across the crest, down another side and then looping back so that it is in front, distantly to your left and surprisingly back on your right. At the top it still melted into the clouds. We walked up the steep stones atop the Wall for a half-mile or so, seeing less as we went. I was satisfied. You can see it, we were told, from the moon. But it is sufficiently breathtaking from here.

The Wall, I learn, is a moral tale. The builder — he actually joined up three earlier walls — was Emperor of the brief Ch'in Dynasty (221–207 B.C.), and he is said to have had 300,000 of the then (it is said) 20 million Chinese at work at one time. This seems not improbable; the stones had to be cut and moved by hand, and the bricks on top were made at a great distance in the plains. And it is some 4000 kilometers (2500 miles) long, not counting numerous flanking, cadet or obsolescent walls, some of which one sees on the way to the Wall itself. Although the cost was heavy, the Emperor would not compromise where national security was concerned. He knew that one should not trifle when survival is at stake. The people did not agree, and the Emperor was overthrown, not by the barbarians from the North but by the Chinese peasants who wanted a reordering of national priorities. Thus the lesson. Wall building against the barbarians continues. Lately we have had the Maginot Line, the McNamara barrier and the row of buses protecting the Republicans at Miami. The Maginot Line, which I once visited, is architecturally inferior to the Great Wall and was militarily no more effective. The McNamara barrier involved

a further and drastic deterioration on all counts. The buses did work but were unimpressive to look at. The preeminence of the Great Wall seems secure.

Some years ago it occurred to me that I had five major sights yet to see in the world — Angkor Wat, all the Egyptian antiquities (which is rather a large package), Petra, the Forbidden City and the Great Wall. (I was insufficiently conscious of the Ming Tombs.) I've done two fifths of the unfinished business in two days.

We spent the afternoon at the Ming Tombs. They lie in a fold of the hills, an hour's drive, also more or less north of Peking. One approaches over an avenue, the Sacred Way, guarded, two by two, by stone camels, elephants, lions, horses and some other better animals not known to nature. Also present and on guard are generals and ministers, much more than life-size, the generals very fierce. The Tombs, with beautifully curving roofs of yellow tile, then lie ahead in a rough semicircle several miles across.

The rooms of actual interment are below; there are great pavilions above. The entrances to only two of thirteen Tombs have been discovered, and only one of the Tombs has been excavated. Judging by the Tomb of the Emperor Wan li, the one who has been dug up, the emperors provided for themselves in an exceptionally spacious way. Wan li's tomb is several stories below ground — the guidebooks speak of it as the Underground Palace. He took with him a fair number of his possessions as no doubt did his relatives and, in contrast with Egypt, there seems to have been no grave-robbing. The valley was

37

Wall: Also a very nice place for jogging

On guard for the Mings and the Thirteen Tombs People's Commune

forbidden ground; the location of the entrance to the Tombs, after it was sealed and covered with earth, was a carefully kept secret, further protected, it is thought, by the precaution of executing those who knew. Thus a great treasure remains to be discovered.

After Wan li we went to see the vast structure of the Third Emperor, Yong le, and the first of the Mings in Peking. You approach through a huge gate to great pavilions almost reproducing the Imperial Palaces. The roof of the main pavilion, the Hall of Eminent Favours, some 220 feet long, is sustained by enormous columns consisting of single trunks of trees of redwood size. They come from Yenan and were, it is said, skidded here all the way on icy roads. Maybe.

Like the Lodis in Delhi, the Mings started building their Tombs long before their death. Wan li got his under way at the age of twenty-two. Again like the Lodis (one assumes), they sensed that it was a task that would be affectionately undertaken by themselves and not by anyone remembering them. The region of the Tombs, once so sacred that the living Emperor was required to dismount before entering, is now cultivated by the Thirteen Tombs People's Commune but the crops are not especially good.

Our day ended at the opera. It was a morality play, well attended. It had to do with the pursuit and capture of bandits by the PLA (People's Liberation Army) in the Tiger Mountains. Strength being lacking, strategy was substituted. Unhappily the strategy, except that it involved getting the bandits drunk, escaped me. One of my companions explained to me the evolution of the opera in China. Before liberation it was only to entertain and amuse; now its purpose is to elevate and instruct. An NBC crew under Lucy Jarvis which is filming the Forbidden City was in adjacent seats. As while gazing at the names carved on the Great Wall, I was struck by how hard it is to be a pioneer anywhere today.

The day, infinitely long, also included a lecture on the political evolution of the University of Peking with special reference to the Cultural Revolution and the revisionist heresies of Liu Shao-chi.

September 12 — Peking

This morning we began a serious, very practical and supremely interesting investigation of the Chinese economy. Research began at a large fresh vegetable and meat market near the center of Peking. It is an area of busy, leafy, narrow streets. Buildings are worn and a bit shabby. The market was clean and devoutly functional and superbly stocked with vegetables, fruit (including melons) and pork. It buzzed with activity; the staff was busy, good-humored and also functional. Prices, even in relation to Chinese wages (of which more later), seemed moderate, and there were no queues. The absence of the latter before scarce items, plus the general aspect of amiability, would greatly impress any visitor from Moscow. It impressed us.

41

The markup on cost is 4.4 percent — around one-fifth that of a workaday American supermarket.[2] Prices are uniform in all markets in the city. They can be changed only with consent of central authority — the local arm of the State Planning Commission. A problem arises here. If the price is too high, vegetables go unsold; if too low, there are queues before they run out. This, like the behavior of water on a hill, is as true under socialism as under free enterprise. The manager states that the problem, the most elementary known to economists, is solved by phoning the supplying communes if the stock seems to be running low, storing if there is too much. Since urban consumption is a small fraction of total consumption, the countryside spares or absorbs as required. Jim Tobin thinks this plausible. I incline to the view that prices — though in some socialist principle not the correct way of rationing food[3] — are more used than this suggests. While higher authority decides what prices are to be, such authority is intelligently susceptible to suggestion as to when abundance requires reduction and scarcity an increase. The keeper of the apple stall, whom I consulted informally, told me that of course apples were reduced in price as the autumn advanced and the supply became more abundant.

[2] This is a tricky comparison. One can never be sure that the margin calculations are strictly comparable. That the Chinese margins are much lower is, of course, not in doubt.

[3] Rationing by physical quantity operates only for rice and its cereal equivalent and for cotton clothing. The basic rice ration varies in accordance with age, work and region. The clothing ration is the equivalent of two suits — trousers, loose blouse, jacket, etc. — a year.

In any case the market was a workmanlike enterprise — busy, affable and with varied, clean and economical abundance. I offer this as a careful and competent judgment.

Next, and at no great distance, we investigated the Peking Department Store. I'm astonished at how much one can learn in a department store. We rather competed on questions — to the Principal Responsible Person and the Chairman of the Revolutionary Committee. Both, their titles notwithstanding, could, I think, easily take over at R. H. Macy's, with only a week's conditioning to the higher executive living standard. Their answers were forthcoming and helpful. After a tour of the store we went for tea and discussion to the Spartan conference room of the establishment.

Here is the Peking Department Store: It has three sales floors, each about half the size of one at Filene's or Saks Fifth Avenue. It is clean, well-worn, hums with activity at midmorning but again with no queues. Presumably because there are no high incomes in China, there is a notable absence of big-ticket items. No furniture, no appliances except for one refrigerator, no television sets but, unfortunately, a growing supply of transistor radios. Turnover is Y (yuan) 200,000 (equaling approximately U.S. $100,000) a day; stock turns over on the average of once every six weeks; the store is open seven days a week from nine until seven. Employees, of whom there are 2300, including 500 in a garment manufacturing plant, average Y63.00 (roughly $31.50) a month with the range being from Y80.00 ($40.00) down to Y36.50 ($18.00).

43

The dollar comparisons are not too meaningful, for food costs are much lower in China than in the United States, clothing expenditures sparse and low, rent nominal, and medical care is provided by the factory or commercial establishment. The store hires about 200 new workers annually; they are recruited mostly from schools in the countryside. No one leaves except as he may be assigned to another job by the state. Executives, i.e., the Principal Responsible Person, the Chairman of the Revolutionary Committee and others, do two days of work a week in a factory. The P.R.P. is forty-two, very plainly, even a bit shabbily dressed, with an attentive, highly intelligent face. Prices are set by higher authority except on products manufactured by the store. Higher authority is, however, responsive to suggestions for change, indicating once again, one imagines, more flexibility in pricing than appears at first glance. Cotton goods are the only items sold by the store that are rationed. Substitutes in the form of rayon are available but are about twice as expensive.

Next comes intelligence which should make Federated Department Stores and all the Lazari blush. The markup is 13 percent on cost; of this the net profit is 7 percent. The markup in the United States for a high-volume department store would be perhaps 45 percent. The Chinese advantages: no slow-moving high-end items, little or no showing of styles, little or no fitting of clothes, high consequent output per salesperson, low returns, no credit, no credit cards, no green stamps, no advertising, no shoplifting. Also no elevators or escalators. The store would not do well in Westchester. It seems right for Peking.

After the Peking Department Store we briefly inspected

*Ming Tomb: Celestial throne
of Wan li unoccupied*

a couple of smaller shops catering to foreign visitors and of no interest. This afternoon we will see an arts and crafts factory. I've declined the ballet for this evening. Slight fatigue. I continue to admire the sparkling, clean streets. This evening I shall find out who is mayor and trade him for John Lindsay, although I imagine they will demand a certain cash consideration. The main streets are lined with multiple rows of trees of recent vintage. The trunks are painted white, and a crew was busy painting this morning as we went into town.

Later

This afternoon we dedicated to the Peking Arts and Crafts Factory, an impressive enterprise employing 1276 people on traditional crafts — pottery, ivory and jade carving, metalwork — of a very high order. Presiding as Principal Responsible Person is a woman who combines great good sense with taste and charm. Many of the craftsmen are surprisingly young; the enterprise combines modern cutting machinery including dentists' drills with traditional handwork. Variations on the old designs are encouraged. Some of the work — a magnificent ivory reproduction of all of the great buildings in the world, each peeping out from ivory foliage — is quite sensational. (Washington, D.C., is present with the Jefferson Memorial, London with Westminster, Rome with the Colosseum. Cathedrals and the Kremlin were evidently excluded from the competition.) I presented the workers with an admirable book on Chinese bronzes which was one of Mrs. Williams's more fortunate acquisitions for my trip. The P.R.P. told us that the only problem is in providing the

46

Peking Department Store.
Patron of shoppers in background

requisite supply of goods. All that can be produced is sold
— mostly abroad. This I do believe.

Later still

After dinner I visited Frank Coe and Sol Adler, two
Treasury friends of New Deal days, expatriated by Mc-
Carthyism. The Coes live in a small but agreeably book-
ish apartment in the Peace Hotel, Sol nearby. Much of
the conversation was reminiscent and personal and, no
doubt, should so remain. Frank urged the easy gift of the
Chinese for organization as the most important factor in
their present economic success. He and Sol guess that the
economy (really industrial and agricultural output) is
growing at the rate of 10 to 11 percent per year, steel production by half as much or more again. Frank stresses the
flexible tendencies of the government in applying rules —
especially in contrast with the U.S.S.R. and Eastern Europe. He supported my interpretation of the vegetable
market. Prices vary substantially with supply and are regularly reduced — sometimes more than once a day — to
clear excess supplies. Other prices are more rigid. Much
latitude on such price matters lies with the municipal
planning authorities. "These prices," he said, "are a great
comfort to all neoclassical economists." Reflecting on the
Cultural Revolution he thinks the estimates of the industrial effects were exaggerated and that the agricultural
damage was rather small. Mrs. Coe told of visiting a
candy factory in Shanghai at the time. The workers were
rather proud of having confined their fighting to the
morning. Then they came back to fill their quotas in the

afternoon and evening. Sadly some windows did get broken.

A pleasant evening.

September 13 — Peking

This morning and the early afternoon belonged to Peking Number 2 Cotton Textile Mill beginning at 8. A.M. My bench marks were the Avondale Mills of Alabama some years back plus a general knowledge of the industry in India. These are not perfect points of comparison but an improvement on the usual situation, which is to see factories in Communist and undeveloped countries that one has never seen in the United States.

Peking #2 CTM is in the suburbs; it is a bit old by Chinese standards (1954–55), employs 6500 and is surrounded by square two- and three-story brick flats which house the workers. The tree-lined streets are by no means unpleasant. We first conversed with the Responsible Persons for Administration, Planning and Political Matters, the latter a good-looking and amiable woman. During the Cultural Revolution the plant was partially disrupted until the PLA moved in to restore order. The union I gather to have been one of the reactionary elements that, along with the technostructure, aroused the antipathy of the Red Guards. It was disestablished. Open shop conditions, Chinese version, have since prevailed but the union is now being reconstituted. Of late, "under the guidance of

49

Chairman Mao's line, workers have gone all out for innovation."

These matters were revealed to us in a large, rectangular room into which we were ushered for tea and a general survey of the operation. The mill makes greige (unfinished) goods only; there are 115,000 spindles and 2400 looms, all made in China. Eighty percent of the product is for domestic use; 20 percent is exported. Some 16 or 17 constructions are made. Orders are given by the Textile Bureau of the relevant central ministry, the name of which I did not get. It specifies each year seven things that are required of the factory, to wit: the value of the product to be produced; the physical yardage; the composition of the physical product; the quality; the required output per worker; the intended profit; the improvement in utilization of materials and labor to be expected over the upcoming year. The rate of profit is 19 percent of sales; the rate of taxation is 21 percent. Both go to the state which obviously does well. The rest is for wages and materials except that the equivalent of 15 percent of the wage bill also goes to the state for retirement, medical care and welfare. Minor replacement of machinery is in the authority of the plant; major capital expansion must be approved by the state. All of this will be most interesting to anyone who owns a textile mill. But it is probably fairly typical of the way light industry in general is operated in China. Wages average Y60.00 ($30.00) a month and range from Y35.00 to Y100.00 with a few older engineers (machinists to us) getting much more. It is the policy to phase in new, younger engineers at wages much nearer to the average. About 70 percent of the working force is women. They work three shifts and a six-day week. The factory closes on Monday partly for maintenance but partly because the rotation of workers to achieve the common seven-day utilization of machinery denies families and friends at the mill a day together. To this they object. (Lenin encountered the same problem.) Closing at this factory is Monday instead of Sunday because of the Sunday crowds at sports events, on buses, in theaters and at parks. Workers who are at a distance from home get two weeks' vacation a year to visit relatives. Travel time is added, and the fare is paid. Otherwise there are no vacations except for national holidays. "We are a developing country and cannot afford holidays," the P.R.P. said firmly.

After our convocation in the big room we toured the plant. Anyone with sufficient curiosity as to what it was like should visit a textile plant. It had a well-used look but was light and clean, and we were accorded a good-humored smile from all, literally all, the operatives. As compared with an American plant, as I recall it, the pace seemed slower, but this is not a conclusion of much competence.

We passed from the cotton bales to the final cloth in about an hour. Exhortation is not lacking. Red flags on a board record the competition between three brigades to improve output. Larger red signs say:

"WE HONOR FOR OUR MOTHERLAND"
"WE HONOR FOR PEKING"

Or at the more practical level:

"SAVE EVERY OUNCE OF COTTON, EVERY INCH OF YARN, EVERY
DROP OF OIL TO SERVE SOCIALIST REVOLUTION AND CON-
STRUCTION."

All of which reminds me that the approach to the plant
was also lined with educational posters including one in
which a worker armed with a wicked-looking ax was giv-
ing the business to the neck of a very damaging capitalist.
The latter bore a remote but still evocative resemblance
to David Rockefeller.

Item: As I have said, rayon is more expensive than
cotton. They would like it to be cheaper (and so intend)
and would like people to prefer it to cotton which they
do not.

From the factory we went to the canteen where lunch
was in progress. If there is any shortage of food, it was
not evident in that kitchen. A battalion of cooks with a
battery of massive cooking equipment was presiding over
a huge and varied quantity of nutrients with a very compelling smell. Workers bring their own mess tins which
are filled beyond all conceivable appetite. Prices in U.S.
equivalents per filling range from five to seventeen cents.

Next we went to the kindergarten which was well prepared for our visit. All visitors to China have remarked on
the uniform for both sexes — shirt, trousers, Mao jacket
where the weather requires. The dress is not, incidentally,
as regimented in aspect as commonly pictured, or perhaps it is one's background. After American undergrad-
uates Chinese workers and students look remarkably well
groomed. In any case the uniform does not exist for small
children. These were customed in a great variety of

bright colors — the girls, in particular, were a bouquet of flowers.

We were treated to a series of entertainments, first by the five-year-olds, then by the six. The five-year-olds featured a fast, competitive game of musical chairs; the six-year-olds provided a concert. We were seated on chairs approximately ten inches in height. A stylish young lady of negligible age came swinging across the floor to bow and announce each number. Then the performers advanced — there were songs and poems in which Chairman Mao was favorably mentioned, a dance featuring the advantages of milk consumption by the young, a ballet based on morning physical exercises, a finale in which the whole class swarmed around and over us. It was most engaging — one of the best concerts I've attended in years. Unquestionably it was rehearsed for our benefit. I am favorably impressed by any society that seeks to persuade visitors by such methods.

After the kindergarten we went back to the canteen for lunch. I gazed over a high wall at more of the kindergarten; they were unprepared, unaware but equally healthy, decorative and — since they were playing basketball and sundry other games — rather more energetic. On the way to lunch we visited a worker's apartment — small, clean, very well furnished and occupied by a woman of fifty-two and her two children. Her mother-in-law was (I believe) adjacent. Both women are retired; the younger because she started work in Shanghai at nine. The retirement age is not completely clear: It is described as fifty for women and sixty for men at 70 percent of the last pay. But apparently healthy workers can and are en-

Peking kindergarten: The juveniles we visited were without uniforms. The book is Mao

couraged to continue in the labor force. This, obviously, could mean many things.

In a small room at the canteen those cooks had gone all out for us. Total effort. Toward the end I counted fifteen different dishes on the table. But then some more appeared. Each was irresistible and was so intended. When it was over, the cooks came in to make sure we were well sated. We were. Like all good cooks they had the aspect of men who had done themselves extremely well. We thanked them to the extent we were able. Then we asked some more questions and, early afternoon, went back to Peking.

Now we are at the University of Peking. My colleagues are reporting to a seminar of some eighty faculty members and students — Leontief on input-output techniques and Tobin on the nature of the available statistical information in the United States. We sit at a long table; four long tables are at right angles. Attention is close and diligent. One translator, alas, has succumbed to our arcane terminology but a second — a professor of English — is performing admirably. I've been talking with another Harvard-trained professor who was a student of Harold Hitchings Burbank. This was another superior preparation for Communism. Burbie was Chairman of the Department of Economics at Harvard for some twenty years from the twenties on. He was another pre-Renaissance man. Though most amiable, he opposed all progress, approved all retrogression. It was said by his defenders that he had redeeming qualities; he was not devoutly anti-Semitic when many at Harvard were, for, being a man of tradition and character, he had not given up being anti-Irish. I sense his student has thrown off some of the influence. He was avid to know who still lived. He had read that I was the economic Richelieu (or Kissinger) behind John F. Kennedy and George McGovern. Tobin (a member of the Council of Economic Advisers under Kennedy, author of McGovern's first welfare program) was far more influential with both. My Harvard friend found this hard to believe. Obviously economic influence is one part action, two parts notoriety.

The meeting is drawing to a close. My colleagues have been clear, concise, interesting. Their audience seems pleased. Tonight the table tennis finals.

A minor point of information from the Coes: Medicines have become very cheap. Common antibiotics are available without prescription. Our highly organized extortion being absent, their cost is nominal. The Pill is free. Frank said, "It's too bad Estes Kefauver [who made cheaper drugs a crusade] never lived to get to China."

A further item: At the close of almost every meeting one is asked for "your criticisms" of the institution or the new China. I've found one that is true, irrefutable and well-received. "You are smoking far too many cigarettes."

The Asian Table Tennis Tournament came to an end tonight in a vast sports arena big enough for a political convention and a probable site for the Republicans if they are in serious trouble four years hence. It was held in the favoring presence of Chou En-lai. The two Ping-Pong tables were quite visible in the distant middle of the distant floor. In the doubles Japanese played Japanese; Koreans played Koreans. In the singles Japanese played Chinese. The singles could be followed, the doubles were

57

Dormitory: University of Peking

confused. In sum the Japanese, as usual, were successful. While I do not need soon to see another tournament, the proceedings definitely had style. I was stunned to discover, when I went out for a stroll, that I knew (or vice versa) some dozens of people in the area reserved for outsiders. Again it is frustrating to one's desire to be the first — as though Columbus landed and was greeted by Norman Cousins. A vast block of seats was occupied by the People's Liberation Army together with the Air Force and perhaps also the Navy. They made a great green, sometimes blue, blanket in one corner of the arena. After it was over, a ballet filled the floor — the latter being the size of several basketball courts. The performers were brilliantly costumed juveniles equipped with large bouquets of flowers with which they pirouetted and danced, finally throwing them into the audience. Speeches were made in Japanese and Chinese (the Japanese also appeared prominent in the management) and after being much too long were translated into English. If table tennis is to succeed as a spectator sport, an arrangement must be made to play it behind magnifying glasses. Otherwise the general impression is of two watchmakers at work in the next town. Their skill is quite extraordinary but soon (especially, as I've said, in the doubles) the scene becomes a blur of arms and legs. This is a minority view. The rest of the crowd followed the action with intense interest and applauded those who won long rallies or brought off fine slams regardless of nationality or, as in the case of the Japanese, previous imperialist condition.

September 14 — Peking

This morning at the University I gave my lecture — a forty-five-minute view of the economic truth as revealed to and by Galbraith. It was in the same room with the same audience as yesterday afternoon's and was to be followed by questions, we of the Chinese and vice versa. When I had finished, the chairman adjourned the meeting, and we learned that we were to tour the University. This we did, beginning with the archeological department. Archeology is visually the most reprehensible of academic sciences; its precincts run to dusty showcases containing arrowheads, stone axes and pottery of repellent appearance in poor repair. The Peking exhibition was normal except for a display which included a facsimile of the Peking Man and several of his relatives. I had not realized how much the Peking Man resembles Mike Wallace. Next we visited a number of the University factories. These, an innovation of the Cultural Revolution, were established to bring workers into closer relation with the University, and vice versa. The shops were in former classrooms and devoted to radio technology of one sort or another. Only a few youngish workers were engaged. They gave us a pleasant handclap but seemed not to be producing very much. The University, seasonally or I suspect otherwise, is at a low level of operations. A library which we later visited was sparsely populated. The economics section treasured a book that I published in 1938. For some decades I have urged strongly against reading it.

Then we went to the Summer Palace only a few minutes away from the University. This was not on my list
of unfinished sightseeing but should have been. Although
on an ancient site, most of the buildings date from late in
the last century when they were restored after being pil-
laged and burned by the British and French in 1860. For
rebuilding, the Dowager Empress used the money that
was meant for a navy. This was superb judgment; the
navy would have been militarily worthless and would not
have survived in any case. The Palace, consisting of many
structures, is spaced out along Lake Kun ming, and the
various pavilions are connected by the Long Gallery of
some 900 yards on the border of the lake. It is open on
the sides; at intervals beneath the roof are paintings of
Hangchow. The lake is itself partly artificial, and the
earth excavated therefrom was used to build the Hill of
Longevity on which are the main pavilions. There are
more pavilions on an island in the lake which, in turn, is
linked to the southern shore by the lovely, upward-curving
Bridge of the Seventeen Arches. Anchored at the far end
of the Long Gallery is a large side-wheeler made of marble; even were it not sitting on the bottom, it is doubtful
if it would be much use as a boat. Still it is beautiful and a
different idea. We took a lighter craft for a tranquil tour
of the lake. The pavilions, palaces, pagodas, all in sun
tempered by slight haze, were a dream. We then had
luncheon at a restaurant in the Palace which, for munifi-
cence, rivaled the one yesterday at the textile mill. My
new meal strategy fell apart. I ate more moderately of
the early dishes. But then it turned out there were twice
as many.

Peking Man: University of Peking

Sadly, at three, we retreated to the University and to the house which once sheltered John Leighton Stuart. The University of Peking is a descendant of Yenching University (a major American benefaction meant to spread enlightenment and Christian principles) of which Stuart was President before becoming Ambassador. It is a lovely house, built in synthetic mandarin, or some such, on three sides of a garden. The door into the garden is flanked by two large cypress trees; the garden is bordered with boxwood, and beyond is bamboo of exceptionally delicate tracery and design. I judge that the original furniture is still in use. Stuart did well doing good. At a long table we had three extremely interesting and thoroughly informative reports on the Chinese economic system — planning, finance, prices — one by a professor and two by members of the Institute of Economics of the Academy of Sciences. They were factual, comprehensive and rewarding. Our Chinese fellow listeners were scarcely less interested than we; one said it was the first time he had had such an opportunity. We and they kept careful notes. It will be more economical to give a rounded conspectus of the Chinese economy when we have finished these discussions. I am now confident, as are my colleagues, that we will have something to tell.

I am very tired, have a headache and am otherwise in need of a deep acupuncture. We start at 8:30 A.M. tomorrow. Only with difficulty did I get from my energetic colleagues, American and Chinese, a postponement from 8:00 A.M.

September 15 — Peking

We did start promptly at 8:30 A.M. and talked until 4:30 P.M., once again in the long room looking out on Leighton Stuart's garden. Today the subjects were agriculture and foreign trade, and again the papers — both by members of the Institute of Economics — were good, especially the one on agriculture. Then came questions. Queries to us about the United States alternated with ours to the Chinese. Any reasonably specific question got a specific answer from the Chinese side. I hope we did as well. We had an hour or so for lunch, again gargantuan. My hosts had learned from a casual remark yesterday that I favored an after-lunch nap so they had a bed ready for me. (Incidentally, our hotel, abandoning the contrivance of the two beds, has constructed a special one. It was nice but not necessary for, if there is room, I fold well.)

The afternoon is now over, and we are about to leave for an evening at the Great Hall of the People.

Item: The hotel houses an eclectic collection of foreign delegations, a majority, one gathers, from Africa. Today a numerous contingent arrived from the Sudan. Most have to do with table tennis.

We have a club, a clinic and a swimming pool. A "brief medical checkup" is required before the pool may be used. The telephone system is by direct dialing — "Dial nine and wait for the dial tone."

Item: A young student in the elevator in the hotel is

studying a section of a book marked RECENT ENGLISH PHRASES. The first phrase in today's lesson: "The plane for Canton has been indefinitely delayed." The second phrase: "The plane to Shanghai has been canceled because of weather conditions."

Later

We are now back from the Great Hall of the People. As Mr. Nixon would say and probably did, it is a very great hall of the people. We arrived a little after six, mounted the outside steps and passed two soldiers, one of whom gave us an amiable smile. Inside we made our way on red carpets through a couple of kilometers of rooms to an elevator and were received on the second floor by President Kuo Mo-jo of the Academy of Sciences. A famous archeologist, now eighty-two, he was an equally famous host. Present were numerous members of the University and Institute of Economics.

The dinner put to shame any minor nutrients Nixon may have had. The conversation, a great many toasts apart, was easy and amiable. I discouraged a discussion of Vietnam, perhaps unnecessarily, with the simple statement that, although we all three were against the war, we thought favorably of the rule of never criticizing one's government outside the country, never ceasing to do so when at home. (The reason, I might say, is not to avoid unpleasantness; it is, if anything, too easy to criticize in sympathetic surroundings. It is, rather, that, if you are quoted, you make yourself less effective at home — and, since your audience is already persuaded, you do not ac-

complish anything anyway.) Japan came up. I said it was
the wish of most Americans to be on good terms with
both China and Japan. Thus we hoped for harmony between the two. Something fairly trite here.

Kuo Mo-jo stressed that China's isolation these last
twenty-five years was not sought — as the Chinese regularly read in Western papers. Especially they were not
keeping to themselves to cultivate those warlike traits celebrated by some foreign statesmen. Could he have meant
Dean Rusk? Rather it was an isolation imposed from
without. This President Nixon had ended. Seventeen
countries have recognized China since the visit; China is
now in the U.N. The Chinese had not expected to make
the U.N. last year, an expectation Henry Kissinger had re-
inforced as he got on the plane to leave last autumn. It
would, they and he agreed, be another year. A few minutes after the plane door closed, they (and presumably
he) got word from New York that both were wrong.

Though not mentioned often, I would judge that Nixon
is running well here. We noted that, while none of us was
a supporter, we all approved his China policy. So did almost everyone else. When Nixon defected, the China
lobby in the United States collapsed.

We discussed further exchanges including the prospect
for Chinese medical and natural sciences missions later
this year — the first such. I would judge the prospect fair
to plus. It seems clear that, once Vietnam and Taiwan are
out of the way, they foresee a good deal of interaction.
"Another three years and you may be tired of Chinese
visitors." As always I think of how casually we handle

PLA man on guard at the Great Hall of the People

visitors in the United States in contrast with the care with which we are being looked after here.

The dinner, having started early, was over at a marvelously early hour. After more photographs — there were many as we arrived — we were on our way home.

Item: In some bland connection I said that many Americans felt we were spending too much on arms and the space race. My hosts were quick to point out that the Soviets were just as bad.

Item: We were blamed for unduly helping the Japanese to recover after World War II. Direct assistance, opening of our markets, use of Japan as a military base. I urged the greater importance of Japan's own efforts and energy. Leontief came down powerfully for the idea that postwar Japan and Germany were successful because they were prevented from using capital for arms. So they had to use it for civilian industry, to our great competitive damage. It is a point with which I strongly agree. I suggested to Fulbright at a hearing a few weeks back that we might arrange to have Hanoi place a similar limitation on our arms expenditure as part of the Vietnam settlement. The idea seems not as yet to have caught on. Maybe the Japanese have put in a request for a new limitation first. They want to stay ahead.

September 16 — Peking

Today a sinus attack. These are headaches, nearly disabling, that leave me stranded between fear that I will

die and alarm that I will not. Several U.S. dollars' worth
of drugs costing, by common repute, five or ten cents here
made me mobile.

At ten by invitation we went to the Foreign Relations Club — an approximate translation — to meet Chiao
Kuan-hua, who is Vice Minister for Foreign Affairs as well
as Chairman of the U.N. Delegation. A dozen or so other
officials were on hand. We consumed tea in a large, pleasant, air-conditioned room. I should have explained long
before now that all meetings in China are conducted over
large covered mugs of tea, constantly replenished.

After opening platitudes we talked about cultural and
scientific exchanges. These were favored. I favor them;
they are also useful, like endorsements of the U.N., as a
way of showing one is a person of superior social percep-
tion and good will. During the last few seconds before
the missiles are exchanged, scholars somewhere will be
proposing closer cultural exchanges as an aid to peace.
Still, I am for them. I extended greetings entrusted to me
by Henry Kissinger, a man, I noted, whose China policy
we approved and whom we were energetically trying to
have thrown out of office. After noting that the Chinese
were not participating in the American elections, the Minister asked me if Senator McGovern would win. I said it
was too early to predict a landslide.

Then he led the conversation on to India. My past in
India has frequently crossed my mind in connection with
this visit. During the border war I was, I prefer to think,
a moderating influence on both the Indian and American
hawks. I put down numerous suggestions for a military
alliance with India and strongly urged the acceptance of

the cease-fire by the Indians. All this was on my theory that it was a border dispute and not an invasion. But I also gave the Indians strong and vocal support. And I arranged for arms and the airlift of troops to NEFA (North-East Frontier Agency) after the Indians had lost everything in the debacle there. I had also found the responsibilities of a war a rather heady business, as middle-aged intellectuals often do. My militant as distinct from my moderating activity was, as usual, the more visible. However Neville Maxwell — whose book is well-known here — may have done something for my reputation as a peacemaker.[4]

The Minister introduced the subject by saying that he had heard that I had been critical of the Chinese veto on Bangladesh. This was not, in fact, so; Jim Tobin had expressed regret. I had expressed doubt that the veto had made a deep impression and sorrow that the matter had been forced to a vote. Bangladesh had more important needs.

The Minister then said that China much wanted peaceful relations with and between India, Pakistan and Bangladesh. However India and "forces back of India" and Mujib Rahman were being intransigent. The Pakistani troops were being held as hostage, the issue of recognition of Bangladesh by Pakistan was being unduly forced. He picked up an earlier comment of mine that this was a difficult time for Bhutto, as for anyone heading a country that had lost a war; accordingly he needed patience and

[4] *India's China War* (New York: Pantheon, 1971). Maxwell concluded, p. 420, that the favorable Indian reaction to the Chinese cease-fire proposal was the result of "some strenuous persuasion by Galbraith." There was such persuasion but as to its effect, I do not know.

help. Bhutto had risked something politically in the uni-
lateral release of Mujib; could those supporting India urge
a more forthcoming position? He made reference to some
new difficulty of the last few days of which I was innocent.
We haven't seen any papers for a week.

I said that friends of India of whom I was unabashedly
one had already made some of his points. As in North
America there is now only one big power on the Asian
subcontinent and a collection of small neighbors. The
small powers face the difficult task of living beside a large
one; the large one must learn to be careful of the feelings
of its smaller neighbors. Both lessons will take a little time.
But no one should imagine that Americans have much influence in these matters. Certainly the Nixon Administration is not one of the forces behind India. Such is its
influence in New Delhi that if it urges peace, the Indians
would think favorably of war. Mrs. Gandhi is, like her
father, an intelligent and highly reasonable leader who
has, of course, to deal with her own politicians. Indian
politics, like that of Pakistan, has a legacy of mistrust and
hatred, as all know. I ventured the guess that this history
is a more important factor in Indian policy than Soviet
influence and agreed that keeping the Pakistani prisoners
— for any reason — was poor policy. All countries —
China, the Soviet Union and the United States — could
do much by not shipping arms to the area.

Chiao then said that the Chinese shared my good opinion of Mrs. Gandhi and my view that, given the power
situation, patience would bring a solution. He was anxious
that they not be considered unfriendly to Bangladesh —
after all, they had enjoyed friendly relations with many

Bengalis. But a greater recognition of Pakistani problems, more flexibility, was essential. Would I convey these thoughts to Mr. Kissinger and my Indian friends? I again noted my lack of omnipotence but agreed.

Leontief invited the Minister to visit Harvard during the U.N. sessions. In supporting the invitation I noted, from personal knowledge, that no diplomat was ever overworked, a remark that evoked great laughing agreement. Chiao mentioned the travel restrictions. I said exceptions were possible and should be sought as a normal procedure — the original restrictions were residues of the Cold War and the Dulles fantasy that the Russians could learn atomic secrets by looking at our corn fields.

At noon, over lunch, we were asked for our criticisms of our program in China, of the University, of whatever else we had observed. Tobin and Leontief urged longer exchanges which means, in general, that younger people be involved. Older scholars are hard to detach, feel obliged for reasons of personal prestige to substitute rapid movement for thought. Tobin asked for more time on an individual basis with responsible and informed people. We all stressed the advantage of seeing officials as well as professors — noting that in the United States visitors seek out the Council of Economic Advisers as soon as (or before) the learned members of the Harvard Department of Economics. I ventured a more delicate point: However important it may be to keep university faculties and students from being a privileged caste, you cannot make first-rate mathematicians, physicists, chemists in a factory. And such people cannot be allowed to waste time when young;

74

they burn out at thirty or forty and then become academic statesmen. We were heard, as usual, with good-humored interest.

My sinus then forced me into bed, and I missed the Temple of Heaven. Later I recovered sufficiently to give an approving comment on our visit to Reuters and the Toronto *Globe and Mail*. Mr. Burns from the *Globe and Mail* was pleased to learn that I had been reared on the old Toronto *Globe* in a community in which no one risked an opinion until the *Globe* had spoken, except where basic truths had previously been established by the same paper. The accepted truths included the beneficence of lower tariffs, prohibition of all alcoholic beverages, private enterprise, public ownership of utilities, an amiable attitude toward the United States, undeviating support of the Liberal Party and an intelligently dubious view of aristocratic pretension in general and that of the British Royal Family in particular. The *Globe* also favored strict economy in conduct of public business. Mr. Burns was not fully aware that he was in such a fine political tradition.

September 17 — Peking to Nanking

At seven last night we boarded a sleeping car for Nanking. A large delegation bade us goodbye at the Peking station — a vast neo-Pennsylvanian structure near the center of Peking. It is of post-liberation vintage. (The skyline of Peking is somewhat defaced by the Stalin–

75

Woolworth-Building style which reaches its terrible apogee in the Hotel Ukraine and the Foreign Ministry in Moscow.) Our train is immensely long, of brightish green with two buff longitudinal stripes. It is full, but not by Indian standards, very clean and pulled by a large, gleaming and very personable steam locomotive. Only two machines have ever had a strong personality — the Model T which was nervous and perverse but determined in a feminine sort of way and the steam locomotive which was solid, good-humored, responsible, masculine but a trifle self-satisfied. Both are gone from the West. The three of us share a comfortable compartment in what resembles an ancient and once elegant wagon-lit. Our companions in luxury seem to be overseas Chinese with possibly some officials. I missed dinner on the train last night (still the sinus); this morning for breakfast we had fruit, ham and eggs, jam, bread, cornbread and coffee. When we had finished, the cook appeared, asking if we approved. I'm reminded that we awoke this morning to a stirring tune coming in from the corridor. I admired it and asked Leontief what it was. He looked distressed but was patient, for it was "The Internationale."

Now for several hours of daylight we have been passing over Chinese countryside. To see things from a train is divine. The rice fields are golden; other crops are green, and just now we are passing some cotton fields with the first white bolls beginning to break. There is corn, very sparse by Coon Rapids[5] standards, and, near the villages,

---

[5] Home of Roswell Garst, once host of Khrushchev and the undisputed king of the whole corn world.

lots of towering, multitargeted sunflowers. The villages here are of gray adobe and thatch, the houses rather larger than in India. Everywhere people are at work in the fields. Virtually all the work — at the moment, rice harvesting — is by hand. Here and there land is being prepared for the next crop; it is by water buffalo, ancient wooden plow and farmer with big conical straw Chinese hat. Where the task lends itself, there is a great deal of gang labor — notably so in the harvesting. The hills of China, which I had always heard of as being bare, are no longer so. Everywhere one sees evidence of the most enormous amount of afforestation —some of it deciduous that I cannot identify, some that looks like Norway pine. In the towns there is much new construction. Leontief and I occupy ourselves by identifying power, chemical, metalworking and other plants. There are many of unrevealed purpose on a great scale. I am surprised at how sparse the villages are. Here — perhaps fifty miles north of Nanking — the land is fairly closely cultivated. By the standards of Bengal, Bihar or Belgium it seems almost uninhabited.

Item: Burns of the *Globe and Mail,* an inordinately thoughtful man, brought us newspapers to the train. This is Sunday, and we have the *Times* (London) and the *Herald Tribune* (Paris) through last Tuesday. Never in my life before have I gone without news for so long. At home it would have been intolerable; it has seemed no loss at all.

Item: In the last village threshing is in progress. Threshers stand around a pile of grain and chaff in the sun-baked square and toss the mixture into the wind. Just before, several farmers in line were wading across a large pond evidently herding fish into a corral. A fish roundup. I hope that's true.

Item: Much more cotton. Not a good crop.

Item: Five ducks stand beside a pond in formation — five ducks in a perfect row.

Later in Nanking

We crossed the Yangtze about noon. To welcome us was the Principal Responsible Person of the Foreign Department of the Nanking Revolutionary Committee, a most agreeable man. The day is warm, not hot; the air and sun are sparkling. Our way to the Nanking Hotel was over long, straight avenues. The plane trees made a complete, shaded arch overhead. There followed a briefing on the economic situation which is favorable. For the moment it is sufficient to say that the industrial output — steel, machinery, machine tools, textiles — has been growing at the pace one detects elsewhere. When Chiang Kai-shek departed to become an American folk hero and the personal archangel of Henry Robinson Luce, Walter Judd and Senator William F. Knowland, the city had thirty smallish industrial plants (including the arsenal) employing 30,000 people. Now 400,000 are employed in some 600 plants. Leontief, who is returning after an absence of forty-odd years, has yet to see anything that then existed.

Still later in Nanking

A gay and charming Sunday afternoon. I remember none better. First we were taken to see the great bridge over the Yangtze. This we had previously crossed on the train. It is double-decked, and at each end two great Y's converge upon it, one arm carrying the railroad, the other the highway. Built between 1960 and 1968, it is not the world's greatest but it remains the major source of local pride. The Yangtze here is about a mile wide, the bridge with approaches a couple of times that long. Sightseeing buses carry sightseers across for a fare of 2½ cents (U.S.). The tower at the end has elevators to the view. We passed into one by an especially massive statue of Chairman Mao and up to a room where a well-knit young woman explained the problems in manufacture of this bridge. There was a shortage of deep-diving equipment but a useful hero — who is celebrated in the room — found a solution that I did not grasp. Then the "Soviets began perfidiously withholding steel [some 100,000 tons] in attempt to scuttle bridge project." Local steel supplies were successfully developed but the attempt by the Russians did nothing to consolidate relations. We went out again by Chairman Mao — he told Edgar Snow shortly before Snow's death that he disapproved of these monuments but his message is not getting through — and toured across the bridge. The valley lands on the other side are rich and verdant; en route we met a large truck stacked with live and very voluble chickens. A train thundered across, shaking the bridge.

Then we drove back through the city — which, with suburbs, numbers some 2.3 million — and out to the mausoleum of Sun Yat-sen. This is too large but is on a beautifully planted and forested hillside and is reached

79

by a total of 392 steps with some intermediate pavilions for rest on the way up. Sun Yat-sen lies below a reclining marble statue with his three principles inscribed on the walls. We paused for the appropriate moment of silence. Then we looked out over the nearby forest, the southern suburbs of the city, an agricultural college and a distant pagoda. A fine prospect. As everywhere, people, who were present in great numbers for a Sunday afternoon outing, waved at us with evident enthusiasm. Some clapped, and some held up babies and pumped their small arms in a special greeting.

After tea — one does not go for more than an hour in China without tea, this being big green leaves in the bottom of the big mugs I have mentioned — we returned to the city but then detoured around the city wall. This, of black brick, dates to the Mings and is in astonishingly good repair. The first Mings ruled from here, and we passed their tombs which are guarded by the same stone animals, the same mandarins and the same fierce and splendid generals as mount duty outside Peking. The generals — perhaps ten feet tall, thick-set and magnificently robed — have expressions of incredible menace. We got by them as fast as possible. What a long way down to Westy! We went to the Xuan wu Lake with its five islands, the latter connected by marble bridges just large enough to accommodate one car at a time, ours being the only ones.

This must be one of the world's most charming parks. It is also well-groomed, and today it was full of people strolling along the walks, passing through the pavilions, looking at the beds of red salvia, strolling over the bridges

80

Pride of Nanking.
This is the big bridge over the Yangtze

or picnicking on the grass. Our ultimate objective was a special pavilion occupied by two giant pandas and one baby version. Our hosts rightly thought it very important that we see the pandas; they greatly approved when we proposed that it was equally important that the pandas see Professor Leontief.

The pandas, both giants and baby, were fine. One looked at us with distaste, got up and ambled inside, and when we followed viewed us with even more distaste. Another paid us no attention whatever; she was on top of a stone column in the cage, seemingly sound asleep. She is, however, a bit of a fraud for, as we watched, she slowly opened one eye and winked. The baby panda was asleep on the wall between the inner and outer cage, one paw trailing down in total relaxation. Presently he woke up and addressed himself to a serious itch in the middle of his stomach. We told of the crowds visiting the pandas at the Washington zoo. Now it is time for yet another ceremonial dinner which, along with all else, memorializes my thirty-fifth wedding anniversary.

Later

Dinner tonight was an extravaganza of regional specialties, each (including the crisp duck and the marinated eels) better than the last. It also developed an interesting discussion on agricultural and regional policy. Agricultural development is not as difficult for an intelligent peasantry as is sometimes imagined. It calls for large-scale use of fertilizers, good seed stock (especially hybrids) that can use the fertilizer, mechanization as needed. If manpower, fertilizer, seed stock are scarce, there must also be willingness to concentrate resources on the good land. The counterpart of agricultural progress in the Middle West, California and elsewhere has been the willingness to allow stony and barren land in New England and poor, eroded or worn land elsewhere in the East and in the Southeast to go back to forest. The Chinese accept the importance of fertilizers, hybrids and mechanization although fertilizer and small tractors are still very scarce. (Fertilizer is being imported from Japan and even from Europe.) They protest vigorously against abandoning areas of low productivity. Instead we were told how one production brigade had transported soil for many miles to make one peculiarly rocky spread slightly productive. Socialist development is held to require this even though (as is claimed) there is presently a labor shortage. It might have been hard to abandon agriculture in New England had it been a matter of deliberate policy. It's an old point. The market can be ruthless as politicians cannot.

After dinner we went to an arts and crafts exhibition just outside the wall. Better work was being done at the factory in Peking. In fact the exhibition was not good. But our hosts were concerned and affable and ended, as usual, asking for criticism. This we refrained from offering. The way back to the hotel at 10:30 P.M. was through leafy, deserted streets that had been crowded an hour before. "Tomorrow is a work day," our guide from the Revolutionary Committee explained.

The Nanking Hotel, also in a pleasantly landscaped

park, is agreeable and efficient but not palatial. I have
a bedroom, sitting room, bathroom and air conditioning.
But that is sufficient.

September 18 — Nanking, Shanghai, Hangchow

After a tranquil night — my first in weeks without addi-
tives — we departed the Nanking Hotel at eight. For our
journeys yesterday three cars about the size of a Swedish
Volvo were produced. After my height had been remarked, a big Red Flag limousine was forthcoming — despite my usual explanations about how collapsible I am.
As we were about to leave, a porter came running out of
the hotel with a look of extreme urgency on his face. He
handed me four Chinese cents — the equivalent of two
American pennies — that had fallen out of my pocket in
my room.

We drove to the station through the town, out through
the wall and across the islands of Xuan wu Lake. I had
not noticed before how vast is the city wall. The original
one, which mostly still exists, was thirty-five miles around
and encircles most of the modern town. A slight mist
hung over the lake, islands and gardens. A pagoda rose
above the cloud. All was fine. Obviously also the land-
scape requires attention to keep it so. Gardeners were de-
ploying widely over the islands, and women were sweeping
the roads and walks. A huge contingent of schoolchildren
— perhaps a hundred in all — were being marshaled along

the walks by their teachers. In contrast with their elders
— as in Peking — their costume included all the rainbow
colors and quite a few that I had not noticed in any
recent rainbow.

Eventually we came to the railroad station; now we are
on the train. Rice terraces, here of lurid green, are on each
side, mile after mile. The villages are more frequent and
the houses, with tile roofs, more substantial. Occasionally
there are patches of cotton, much not good. Just now, by
a pond, a large group of workers were filling pails. Others
were on their way with their cargo, two pails on a yoke,
evidently to moisten fields above the irrigation ditches.
We've yet to see the first tractor. We do see many more
new industrial plants and much building in the towns. As
we get closer to Shanghai, cotton replaces the rice, and
the pickers, in groups of twenty or more, are moving across
the fields. It is a little like the old South but not much.
It's ever so much tidier.

Later — Shanghai station

We pause for a half hour here. The railroad station is
still the center of activity in a Chinese city. In an American city no one any longer knows where it is. A prominent feature of the scene, everywhere in China, is the
PLA. Members wear a clean, remarkably shapeless uniform of grass green with a soft, peaked cap. Except for
red collar tabs and the red star on the cap, it is the garment
of a fairly casual motor mechanic. Footwear runs from
sneakers to sandals to cloth-top shoes. Both sexes are en-
rolled, and the uniform — like much though not all work

clothing — is the same for both. There are no insignia of rank. The men know their own officers; others need not know and can only judge by age and bearing. One of our three colleagues from the University of Peking who is accompanying us remarks that he can make a close estimate as to who is an officer but he cannot be sure. Any reflection on the number of military men in a community is highly misleading. In China as in numerous other countries they wear uniforms off duty. In other countries, including the United States, they do not. But there are many here.

Jim Tobin has committed the journey to learning Chinese chess and teaching the Western or Fischer version. He has won great respect for both.

Later — Hangchow

We arrived here a bit after five and were given a warm welcome by the Responsible Person of the Foreign Affairs Department of the Hangchow Revolutionary Committee and the head of the local Scientific and Technical Association. I have a feeling that whoever was in charge before the Cultural Revolution was usually designated head of the Revolutionary Committee — that there has been more continuity than the name implies. Had the revolution come to Harvard, Nathan Pusey would doubtless have gone, but in New Haven Kingman Brewster would still be Chairman of the Yale Revolutionary Committee. A large crowd — several hundred — had gathered to welcome us, attracted less, I fear, by our fame or authority on economic questions than by the huge car with curtains that awaited us outside the station. They returned our waves and cheered Leontief's photographic effort with gusto. Then we went through the city which was full of homeward-bound cyclists and pedestrians and out on the wide avenue that borders the Western Lake. The sun, large and very red, was setting behind the distant hills. The water was smooth, utterly serene. Again the haze and distant pavilions and pagodas. I was brought back to reality by my host. He asked if I hadn't been made familiar with the scene by television during Nixon's visit. I had to explain that I had been away from home and negligent.

Item: I've earlier noted the resemblance between South China and Bengal. Approaching Hangchow the similarity is striking. One passes field after field of tall jute — a noble plant — with, of course, much rice and many mulberry trees.

Item: Tobin observes that there are no dogs or cats in China. The reason is presumably economic; if food has been scarce and rationed, affection for a participating pet must diminish. This seems especially probable if the pet is itself edible.

September 19 — Hangchow

Morning in Hangchow. We depart at eight by boat from in front of our hotel for a journey over and around one of the larger sections of the Western Lake. Our vessel is a big motor launch of deliberate pace; we sit aft around a tea table over mugs of tea. Everything favors the journey; the sun is warm with a gentle haze; the distant hills are still mysterious and lovely. Seven hundred years ago this was the most famous resort in all the world; there is still nothing to rival the marvelous sweep of tranquil water, the islands, bridges, causeways and pavilions. Everything has been downhill from 1276 to Miami Beach.

We pass the pavilions, some jutting into the water, with red columns and curving tile roofs. Between are willows in a row without end and flowering peaches. People stroll on the terrace that runs along the water; in the distance we see the steeply pyramidal Bao Shu Pagoda. Some very large, very fat fish jump out of the water in the wake of the boat. Fish abound; the guide tells us that the revenues of the fishing brigade help pay the cost of maintaining this grandeur. We continue by a hotel for overseas Chinese and later see many of the clients; they are easily identified by their bright unorthodox clothes and their much more luxurious bottoms. Our guide says a few come from the United States but most — I suspect nearly all — are from Hong Kong, Singapore and elsewhere in Southeast Asia. Nothing keeps a bona fide resident of Hong Kong from getting a visa and visiting the ancestral scene, and many do.

We have now traveled for half an hour or so, and the lake is dotted with canopied boats — usually one man paddling in front, one behind, a largish passenger list relaxing in between. Earlier we went by Solitary Hill; now we pass the promontory of "Orioles Singing in Willows" and come to an island which encloses a lake in which there is an island. It is called, correctly, "Island within an Island." We disembark and wander along paths and over high-arched bridges below which are pale pink water lilies and strong reddish-pink lotus. Just beyond the island three small stone towers rise from the water. They are "Three Towers Reflecting the Moon." During the autumn festival they are lit and valuably supplement the moon. On the other side of the "Island within an Island" our boat is waiting. We stop before a fairy-tale pavilion to take some pictures. As usual a large crowd is attracted by the Polaroid. We pose with our companions; the picture is snapped; Jim Tobin pulls on the film, and everything disintegrates. The crowd looks disappointed; Edwin H. Land, of all people, has failed. I ask Jim to explain that such failures are part of our system and to mention the C5–A. He declines. The next picture is completely distinct, our technology vindicated. We board the boat and pass on to the "Flower in the Pond" garden featuring huge and voracious goldfish and then on to the Peony Pavilion featuring, not surprisingly, peonies which are gone and flowering trees which are still bright. Fifty or so children of twelve or thereabouts are busy weeding a bank and make an ostentatious point of not being interrupted as we pass. We are taken to view a tree, one of four contributed by President Nixon on his visit. It looks to survive.

It develops that we have passed from the islands to the mainland, and our cars are waiting. The next stop, past some tea gardens, is the Liu He Pagoda, 1002 years old, with a sweeping view of the Qian tang River and the railroad bridge to Foochow and the south. In the past a

On the Western Lake

tidal bore coming up the river from the East China Sea caused great distress to the city at certain high tidal seasons. The first public works effort, though supplemented strongly by prayer (the problem being deemed beyond human strength) proved inadequate. Then in 910 the Governor, Qian liu, later King of Wu Yue, set about seriously building the definitive wall. He had great trouble, for each tide washed away what had just been accomplished. But he hit upon the plan of stationing archers in a row on the unfinished dike with instructions to shoot at the top of the waves as they rolled in. This worked; the wall was completed and it still stands.

From the pagoda we went to a cluster of pavilions on a hillside. By the highest of the pavilions is Tiger Spring. The spring traces back to a monk who appeared in the vicinity a considerable time ago, rejoiced in the beauty of the location but then discovered there was no water. He appealed to a couple of friendly angels who happened along, and they told him that God would look into the matter. And next morning He did: two tigers appeared, dug industriously into the hillside and found water.

We went into one of the pavilions where we learned about the remarkable quality of this water. A waitress demonstrated. You can fill a tea bowl with it, not full but heaping full. And then you can float coins on the gently upward-curving surface. We had tea made from this talented water, and it was time to come back to the hotel for lunch.

Much later in Hangchow

This afternoon we explored the Ling Yin Temple — really two, one guarding the other. They are Buddhist and huge. The first centers on a smiling Buddha with a superb stomach that one of our companions from Peking said he believed Americans called "a beer belly." Right. In the second and larger temple is a yet larger, benign and didactic Buddha who, in fact, towers to sixty feet. At the back of the Buddha is a relief of incredible complexity, also rising into the crown of the temple. The central feature is a largish Buddha standing in the ocean on the head of an even larger fish. From a jug in his hand he is replenishing the ocean. It is an imaginatively conceived operation. Lined up protectively on either side of the great Buddhas are gods, ministers, scholars and generals, the latter as usual with terrifying scowls. Altogether they are a fine pair of temples, set in a rocky glade. We learned that R.M.N., ill-advised as so often, did not make it but — and I quote — "Pat came."

Next we looked at the Jade Fountain, a modern effort at garden architecture. The distinguishing feature of the spring is the large black fish — some almost a yard long — that patrol the basin into which the water flows. They are shaped like U-boats, which they otherwise greatly resemble, and are truly sinister.

Then came the Yellow Dragon Cave, which has a yellow dragon on the side of another rocky glade. He breathes water down on the rocks below. Here we learned about bamboo breeding and culture, a subject none of us had previously encountered. Some well-bred species grow four or five inches a day and reach a diameter of six or eight inches in a single year. Then they grow no more. There is also under development a square bamboo. And bamboo with one flat side. These will be handy for construction. Also purple bamboo and bamboo of alternating colors along the stem. There is far, far more to bamboo than one thought. The small forest where all this is happening is serene and lovely.

Then we passed the University and went back to the Western Lake where we climbed Solitary Hill (which our guide now calls Isolated Hill) for a view of the site of an old summer palace of the Mings. Nothing remains. We had tea at a pavilion down by the lake. Jim Tobin drew a crowd of a hundred or so to watch him take a picture of a compelling child of about three. He gave her the picture; she gave Leontief her fan.

Then we went back to the hotel, were seen away with great courtesy, dined handsomely on the train and at 9 P.M. were in Shanghai. A large delegation was on hand to meet us. We are now ensconced in the Beautiful River Hotel, fairly new, fifteen stories and very solid. It is perhaps a mile from the erstwhile Bund — the great commercial street fronting on the Whampoa River — down but well off Nanking Road. I occupy a suite that, for its grandeur, causes my colleagues to call me Chairman. It may be a misnomer. According to Edgar Snow, Chairman Mao's tastes are more conservative. Grand or not, it is exceedingly comfortable.

94

September 20 — Shanghai

Morning tea arrived at six today. I had slept so well that I welcomed it. Outside and below a game of basketball was already taking form. At eight we met with our hosts to discuss our program. We added a "middle school" and a hospital to our previous list of requests or prospects, these being the University, a commune, a big industrial establishment. All seems by way of being arranged.

First this morning, however, we went to the permanent industrial exhibition. It is in the former Palace of Sino-Soviet Friendship. The architecture must have put an added strain on that friendship. It is the nadir of deteriorated Stalin gingerbread with more than a trace of Rayburn Building elephantiasis.

The exhibition, for which we had informed and highly intelligent women guides, establishes to my satisfaction that there is nothing much that China does not make. In the great main hall, Marx, Engels, Lenin and Stalin at one end, Chairman Mao between ten furled red flags at the other, we saw a turbo-generator, 300,000-kw inner water-cooled, stator and rotor model; cold extruding machine; five-color rotary gravure press (Model 5-S WJ-801); an industrial digital computer, also called Calculateur Numerique, Industriel Model TQ-3; a 12,000-ton hydraulic free-forging press; a Laser Dynamic Balancing machine. There was much more but at this point the products became a bit technical and I did not always grasp their purpose.

95

Then we looked at the models of ships launched in recent years including dry cargo carriers of up to 25,000 tons (tankers have not exceeded 15,000, we were told) and a somewhat smaller freighter with the excellent name of *Sun-in-the-Morning*.

Automobiles are made in Shanghai, and the display included a wonderful black convertible in which dignitaries can ride on a specially elevated seat. When there are no dignitaries, the seat retracts. The farm machinery exhibit included tractors of various sizes up to 45 hp (diesel) but was sparse.

Next we passed on to the light industry section where, among the other products of light manufacturing, was an automatic acupuncturing machine. Here also we saw a film of a lady undergoing heart surgery with acupuncture anesthesia. Her heart pumped away in a rather confusing mass of bloody tissue over which the surgeons worked with apparent knowledge. All this was kept out of her sight. She was, however, fully conscious. Her face registered no pain but a certain understandable anxiety. Before being shown the film we were, according to rule, asked if the sight of blood troubled us.

There were numerous silks, synthetics and cottons. I came to understand textiles when I was a price-fixer — their prices were among the hardest to fix. For some curious reason, looking at them still gives me pleasure. Perhaps it is the thought that I will never again have to see Robert Ten Broeck Stevens or any other textile manufacturer. In World War II they were, with the cattlemen, the most voracious of entrepreneurs. The cheapest sewing machine costs $75, the best around $125. A good Shanghai watch costs about $30; a reliable Nanking model, $15. The bicycle display looked fine with one ten-speed model. Portable typewriters are available for English and Chinese. The latter must select from some 1500 characters with another 1500 in emergency reserve. The Chinese have invented a disturbing gadget which plays records, receives radio and broadcasts to a loudspeaker. It costs, I regret to say, only $65. There was much more including a Cardiac Defibrillation and Pacemaker unit, the "Jing-lieu Jing-Xue" glass man whose body shows the 361 points where acupuncture may be made, and a lively collection of mechanical toys. The most advanced of these was a hen that shoved two chicks around in a perambulator while laying eggs at intervals as she proceeded. Toward noon we said goodbye to our intelligent and charming guides and came back to the hotel. We now learn that the school and hospital are for this afternoon.

Item: In the United States the automobile has driven the pedestrian and bicycle from the streets. Its victory is total; in consequence the noise of battle has greatly subsided. In China the struggle for the streets is still on; the issue is far from resolved even if the ultimate outcome is not in doubt. The rare automobiles and the numerous trucks blare constantly at the cyclists and pedestrians. The latter still resist. Traffic noise in Shanghai is thus far louder than in Boston or New York.

Later

The afternoon was a joy and unalloyed success. It took us first to the Tsao Yang Number Two Middle School in industrial Shanghai — a zone of peach stucco and mud-

97

gray brick flats, shopping centers with one that had undertones of a supermarket, and through throngs of pedestrians and cyclists and a few surviving pedicabs. Our driver had difficulty locating the school. Though word of our arrival could not have reached the school before midmorning, it was well prepared; a red sign at least thirty feet long and a yard high proclaimed "Welcome to the American Economists." Another smaller sign in the main hall affirmed the message.

We were greeted by the Chairman of the Revolutionary Committee of the school, the Vice Chairman, the PLA representative (a most congenial looking warrior) and the student head of the Red Guards, a girl of fourteen or fifteen, slender with braided hair and a face of ceramic beauty. A Red Guard! My illusions were all too few before.

We were taken for tea and welcoming speeches to a room with a long, lace-covered table. The Chairman, who had been in office for seven years and so evidently had undergone only terminological reform with the Cultural Revolution, gave us the central statistics: 2400 students of very roughly our high school ages; 120 staff; 900 such schools in Shanghai and suburbs (500 in the city); a six-day week; six hours of classes a day; nine basic subjects, these being politics, Chinese languages, English, Russian, chemistry, agriculture, history, revolutionary art and literature. (Something must be missing here for we then moved out to visit classes and the first was mathematics.) The school is of two-story brick with grim concrete interior walls and floors and large crowded classrooms. There

98

提高警惕 保卫祖国

87098.

were fifty or sixty to a class. The mathematics class featured a spirited exposition of logarithms by the teacher; the English class involved responsive reading about the celebration by the people of Shanghai of Chairman Mao's swim (they seem to have jumped wholesale into the Whampoa); a literature class featured recitation. The responsive reading was a determined and energetic performance audible for up to fifty yards. All three teachers were men.

Then we looked at the school factories — which were turning out small but serious quantities of sodium pyruvate, cupric tartrate, wooden soap (packing) boxes and metal transformer parts. The production was more impressive than at the University of Peking. This is work experience which — factory, farm and military — accounts for 30 percent of the students' time. Seventy percent is "intellectual" training.

Next came recreation in the adjacent fields and a large shedlike gymnasium back of the school. The sports were volleyball and table tennis, some of the latter at a supraprofessional level. Even close up I could barely follow the ball. Tobin pleased everyone by trying out unsuccessfully for the team. Finally there was a concert — the last stages of a rehearsal for the upcoming National Day celebrations. A ballet by a dozen teen-agers, beautiful, mobile and very energetic, celebrated support for Chairman Mao and then the close relation between students and the PLA. It was done with great vivacity and considerable grace. Back with the tea and lace tablecloth we asked more questions, answers to some of which are above. I asked what subjects the students liked best. My lovely young friend from the Red Guards said that all students liked all subjects for all helped to build a better country. For her part she had a slight preference for Chinese history because of the way it raised political consciousness.

This school brings up questions that cannot be easily answered. Obviously it is an instrument of the most formidable discipline, political and otherwise. Equally without doubt, and partly because of the discipline, it is a highly effective way of getting maximum high-school-level instruction from very limited resources. All students in Shanghai now complete secondary schooling — "It has been popularized." After the usual picture-taking and speeches we departed.

The Hoa Shan Hospital, which dates from 1907, has of late been much enlarged. We met first for tea in the pavilion of a pretty garden that had once belonged, conveniently enough, to a neighboring English capitalist who built it for a tubercular daughter. It is now used by the patients. An old and handsome Victorian building is supplemented by a huge medical factory in Alcatraz Modern. Patients pay (in approximate U.S. dollars) $0.50 daily for a bed, $0.15 for food, plus the cost of medicine and surgery. A minor operation such as an appendectomy costs $5; major surgery such as lung removal costs $15. An outpatient call is five cents. However all industrial and government workers are covered by insurance plans so these figures overstate the cost for the average citizen. Mothers stay in the hospital a week after childbirth, get 56 days' maternity leave with pay.

We were given a run-down on the public health situation by one of the older staff members — he spoke English and with the quiet authority of an old medical hand. Shanghai has about one doctor to a thousand people. Venereal diseases have disappeared; they have not seen a case of either syphilis or gonorrhea for several years. Infectious diseases have been greatly reduced and continue to decline. Cancer, heart disease and industrial accidents (despite safety precautions and training of first aid personnel) are increasing. Thus the march of civilization. In the case of cancer and heart disease, something must be attributed to better diagnosis.

We visited a ward devoted to accident repair — and were shown around by a woman doctor whom one would trust. The hospital has 600 beds, 150 staff, of which (I believe) 60 are women. As a teaching hospital it also draws some medical support from its affiliated medical college. A specialty is replacing fingers, when all or most are lost, with one of the inner toes which isn't especially needed. We examined a man with such repair in progress; the former toe was not beautiful but looked very functional to me. I gather the operation is one of some delicacy. As with everything the ward was unfancy but scrupulously clean. Except in the rooms where hands were being repaired we were given the usual vigorous handclaps.

Tonight we went to see the Shanghai acrobats, jugglers and magicians. The theater was full; we sat between a delegation from a Scottish friendship society and another from the British Amalgamated Engineering Union. The audience was highly appreciative and so were we. The show began with some extremely talented calisthenics;

then a bevy of handsome girls twirled saucers at the end of bamboo poles. One, only slightly more deft than the rest, twirled five in each hand while standing on a bench balanced on a teacup. Twelve people rode a bicycle hardly big enough for one; a man balanced three eggs on the end of a poker held in his teeth, then broke one egg in a bowl and brought out a chicken. In general the idea was to make things as difficult as possible. The unionists recognized me from BBC on which I did a series of broadcasts a year or so ago; one leaned back and said: "That's the kind of bloody precision work that busted Rolls-Royce." They also said that they had found Chinese engineering work on brief inspection very competent if not yet up to British or United States standards. Tomorrow a People's Commune very early.

Item: In line with the industrial safety program mentioned above, the acrobats whose work takes them to the top of the stage wear safety belts. It must be easier on their nerves, as it was on mine.

Item: In conversation with the doctors yesterday Leontief asked, good-humoredly, if there was scholarly conflict between the practitioners of Western and traditional Chinese medicine in Shanghai — there are 8500 of the first, 3000 of the second. He was told there was not. Chairman Mao had told them to cooperate. At about this time I was extracted from the discussion to have my throat examined. Not oratory but a rapidly developing cold was causing trouble. My doctor, a tall, handsome woman who spoke perfect medical English, said I would survive. She prescribed a limited dose of some Western pills and a much larger dose of traditional herbs, also compressed into pills.

Item: Medical services are badly distributed between town and country as might be imagined. Since the Cultural Revolution our hospital has dispatched 15 medical teams to outlying and border areas. One, in the course of a year, gave 20,000 treatments, performed 1000 operations "under primitive conditions" and trained numerous "barefoot doctors" for rural practice.

September 22 — Shanghai

A day is missing for reasons presently to become known. Yesterday morning, starting at eight, we made our way through the endless urban wastes of Shanghai, out into the suburbs and on into the countryside. It was another sparkling autumn morning; our three cars did battle as usual with the pedestrians and cyclists. However so few are the cars as yet that we are allowed to turn or cross on red. Only the trucks (and bicycles) must observe.

Beyond the city and suburbs our way led through rice, vegetable and cotton fields. On one side beyond the first fields was a canal. At intervals of a few hundred yards were cement pillboxes, brown and aging but immortal. Chiang's armies built them to defend the approaches to Shanghai. There are literally hundreds of them. Whatever its other shortcomings, the Kuomintang army was unparalleled on pillboxes. One of my companions, mentioning them, said that Chiang Kai-shek was known in the Communist armies as "our Transportation Leader." He arranged for the transportation of much-needed weapons from the United States. Then his soldiers obligingly made them available to the Red forces.

On the canal, as we drove on, was a procession of boats, each with a high, square sail. The sails looked as though they were passing through the rice or cotton. A brisk wind was blowing down the canal. Some of the boats had their sails filled on one side and were moving in that direction. Others bulged on the other side and moved against the wind. Later I asked one of my new friends about it. He said that with revolutionary energy anything was possible. He also added that it might have been an optical illusion.

After an hour we arrived at the Hsu Hang People's Commune in Chia Ting County and were greeted by the Vice Chairman of the Revolutionary Committee and also the Responsible Person for the enterprise. The established routine was followed: first a general survey of operations, then a tour, then a return for tea and more questions. All this took all morning and was exceedingly instructive.

I doubt that Hsu Hang is a wholly typical commune. There is a tendency in such matters to mislead. Our next-door neighbor in Dunwich Township, Elgin County, Province of Ontario, in my youth was Bert McCallum, a most amusing and kindly man and everyone's friend. He was not a good or energetic farmer. The Agricultural Representative (County Agent) never took important visitors from the Ontario Department of Agriculture to see Bert's farm. It was, on the whole, more typical than ours to which the great men did come. However I asked the Vice Chairman of the Revolutionary Committee if he had many visitors. He said he did not. Like every Chinese manager we have encountered, Mr. Chen was young, obliging, informed and intelligent. He would do well anywhere.

The Hsu Hang People's Commune has 4694 households, 20,500 inhabitants and 1688 hectares (roughly 4200 acres) of land, all irrigated. This, it will be seen, is no great amount of land — less than an irrigated acre per family. The crops are grain (two crops of rice a year plus one of wheat), cotton, hogs and a variety of factory enterprises. With total grain output now at 12,015 kg. a hectare (and 2.2 times the 1957 level) the commune has a grain surplus. When first organized — and with only two yearly crops, wheat and rice — it had to import grain. Cotton production is 540 kg. per hectare, ginned basis. (That involved some translation problems. There seems to be no word for gin.) Small factories turn out about Y5.4 million worth of goods annually — around $2.7 million — and produce half the total revenue of the commune.

The working force of the commune is divided into 11 production brigades and these, in turn, into 121 production teams — the latter being the basic production unit of the enterprise. Last year the commune, after taxes, production costs (other than labor) and reserves for welfare and investment, had an income for distribution of Y155 (about $75) per capita which works out to Y675 (about $335) per household. The Hsu Hang Commune is, by Chinese standards, highly mechanized — 22 tractors of 35 to 45 hp and 62 smaller ones of 12 hp or less. This must be far above the average although later, when we asked the main need of the commune, the Vice Chairman said it was for more mechanization as well as better agricultural techniques. Fertilizers are 70 percent organic, 30 percent chemical. The first consists of hog manure, local night soil and organic waste shipped out from Shanghai. The chemical fertilizer is used on both wheat and cotton. It is, I believe, very scarce. The cotton could, I judge, use a lot more.

So much, once more, for facts. We now started on a tour of the premises. First a house — really three houses, each of two rooms around a tiny brick courtyard. These, old and with dark gray tile roofs and stone floors, had some charm. Around them were the private vegetable plots, very tiny, which, I'm prepared to believe — as we were told — do not produce much surplus for sale. The bedroom featured dramatic mahogany beds, some more or less completely enclosed in the manner of a large sedan chair. Adjacent were some new apartments — two-story brick, decent, a little smaller if anything than the old and lacking all the older grace. But they too are scrubbed. As compared with Indian villagers the Chinese are blessed more than they know by the absence of cows and cow dung.

The hog operation which we next visited was unimpressive. An effort is being made to improve the local stock by crossbreeding. I believe it needs it. (My competence in these matters is aging but adequate. My first degree was in animal husbandry. I was once on the judging team of the Ontario Agricultural College at the International Live-stock Exposition in Chicago.) Ownership of hogs is widely distributed — the families we first visited, in addition to their private plots, also had their personal pig. Then we went to the factories. These, including some we did not see, make elementary threshing machines, furniture, bas-ketware, boxes, light bulbs, chemicals and steel pipe. The factories are small — at most a few dozen workers in those we saw — and there is not much attempt at line produc-tion. Men and women are mostly either making a whole item or a substantial component.

Still they are serious operations — not a show. The jus-tification is not efficiency but the employment of labor that would otherwise have little to do — technically it is the Chinese answer to one of the greatest problems of rural Asia, that of recurrent and disguised unemployment. The latter consists of two people doing what one could accomplish; remove a worker and production does not fall; the effective marginal product is zero. Even ineffi-cient production, therefore, improves on the existing sit-uation — always assuming it can be organized, which the Chinese seem able to do. (Other countries have tried and failed.) Also there may be some value in the teaching of technical skills and discipline. I will return to this prob-lem when I survey the economy as a whole. At each fac-tory during our pilgrimage we received the usual amiable handclaps from people who then went promptly back to work. One is expected to clap back. That is an expecta-tion aroused, evidently, by the Russians. I wave. One must take a stand.

Commune interior—clean, decent, grim.
This house is near Peking

The commune has four middle schools (the first two years of which are compulsory), twelve elementary schools and a hospital of twenty beds. We visited the latter, very plain, very functional, very clean with an elementary operating room and a dentist who was standing invitingly beside his chair.

Back at headquarters we had tea and a circumstantial review of the finances of the commune. Of the total product, 6 percent goes for taxes, 25 to 30 percent for costs of materials, 5 to 7 percent for capital accumulation and welfare, 1 to 2 percent for management. The remaining 55 to 63 percent is distributed to the members. This distribution must make for some interesting times at Hsu Hang. The first division is between the production teams, this being in accordance with their contribution to product. That is relatively straightforward. Each team member then participates in accordance with his recorded hours of work as modified by his accumulated points. These, on a scale from 0–13 per day, are based on (1) his skill and technique, (2) his physical strength and (3) his work attitude — "whether hard or lazy." The points are to ensure that he is paid according to *both* the quantity and quality of his work.

A record is kept of each team member's hours. Then members assemble once a month to discuss and establish their point ratings. Each worker proposes his own rating. It is then adjusted in discussion. The rating established, the shares follow. The commune is not a welfare organization. If a man is sick, he gets no share; if aging parents have children, the latter must provide. Only the childless old are a charge on the community.

Recently, a ninety-eight-year-old woman died; she had outlived all her descendants. So in latter years she had been rotated around daily for feeding to members of the production team. There is a similar American system by which families look after aged ancestors by shipping them around from one son or daughter (and respective reluctant spouse) to another. Neither system seems perfect.

We asked if there was provision for appeal from the team's decision on points. Here I got the impression that the excellent and forthcoming Mr. Chen may have resorted to tact. He said that the problem did not ordinarily arise; people knew each other's performance well and thus the points were easily decided. Usually workers proposed scores for themselves that were too low. They were raised in common discussion. But occasionally someone suggested too much for himself. By discussion he was brought down to his proper position. So be it. It is an arrangement that could risk the Harvard syndrome. This is the tendency of professors, conscious that their promotion depends primarily on the good opinion of their peers, to improve their chances by discreet but ubiquitous self-praise. A terrible thing.

It was one before we were back at the hotel; by 2:15 P.M. we were again in motion en route to the Shanghai Machine Tools Factory.

This time we passed along the Bund. The great, solid Victorian buildings, denuded of their signs, have a vacant, heavy, forlorn look. We've heard that the upper floors of some of the old imperial skyscrapers are unused. Feudal palaces are visited by the masses but not the one-time offices of the Hong Kong and Shanghai Bank.

111

The Bund in Shanghai: British lion still fights back

The SMTF was far out on the edge of the city and was a grim and busy expanse of machines building other (mostly grinding) machines. Women work along with men. Only machine tools reproduce like people. The parent machines as well as the offspring were nearly all Chinese. Six thousand people were at work in ten workshops of which we saw two. I know almost nothing about such operations; I was visiting a type of plant that I had only once (in Springfield, Vermont) visited in the United States. Accordingly I left the questions to my two colleagues who were under the same handicap.

After the plant tour we went for tea and discussion with our hosts. Not much was accomplished. This plant, a favorite of Chairman Mao, has grown hugely in output and technical complexity of products in recent years. A truly formidable effort is being made to grade up the working staff. There is a plant college; especially competent workers are dispatched elsewhere to study engineering; management, engineers and operatives are exhorted to work together for greater effect and may well do so. Of the 300 engineering and technical staff, 150 have been brought from the ranks. Discussions of costs, margins and profits eventually disintegrated into confused noncommunication.

I later learned more about the shop, secondhand, from the Amalgamated Engineering delegation who were there yesterday. They were impressed and precise. "I'd say it's up to where we were in 1957." Two other comments from the same source: "How about all those women running machines?" And "I tell you, those lads really work. Too hard. They'll beat us out yet."

I asked "What would you do about it? Organize?"

"You said it, Professor. You said it!"

One reason for my negligence at the Shanghai Machine Tool Factory was the increasing sense that I was burning up — even in the room where air conditioning was needed for precision work. My lungs hurt. At one juncture I wondered if, accidentally, I had inhaled several of the steel billets at the foundry. Back in town they took me to the hospital (another hospital), and I rode up in the elevator with an elevator operator in a white coat with a stethoscope sticking out of his pocket. He took me along the hall to an office and proceeded to examine me. He was also the doctor. The examination was thorough — roughly what Prudential requires for half a million. He told me some kind of infection was invading me, raising my temperature and blood pressure. He pushed aside the drugs from yesterday (including the herbs) and gave me three new kinds including a most authoritative antibiotic. He asked my guide if we would walk down. Another patient was in need.

Still remaining was a ceremonial dinner by the Scientific and Technical Association of Shanghai, a most detailed affair featuring napkins shaped like flowers, one dish decorated with a nightingale carved from a pumpkin, soup served from watermelons decorated with elaborately carved friezes and a succession of some fifteen or twenty dishes, each more complex than the last. All were rotated on a giant lazy Susan at the center of our huge round table. There were many, many toasts. I could eat little and drink nothing.

Thus the missing day; I staggered into bed and slept

intermittently. This morning there was a session at the University. I had to give up and go back to bed. I'm now much better. But the charge of the bacteria, the counter-charge of the antibiotic, the sanguinary fighting incidental to it all, have left my insides devastated like the Western Front after Arras.

Later

My recovery has been rapid. I went out for a drive and to buy some silk. It is in unlimited supply with a pleasant range of designs at around U.S. $2.50 a wide yard. We leave at 6:30 P.M.

Later still — Out of Shanghai

All airports are the same; the compulsion to make the ceiling unnecessarily high, the metalwork unduly bright, transcends ideology. So with the Shanghai airport which we left with much ceremony and no red tape an hour or two ago. Air France had yesterday's *Herald Tribune* aboard; it was the first news since the Burns endowment dated a week ago Tuesday. No radio, no television, no newspapers, no word-of-mouth. A mimeographed news-sheet from the wire service is distributed in Peking but not to our hotel. Letter bombs seem to be the only new advances in the civilized arts during the ten days. Again I was struck by how easily one accommodates, though after a time, presumably, one would get out of touch. The Chinese have. At the University today, a student evinced doubt when Leontief told him that, in the United States, the poor could also vote.

Item: On the way to the hotel yesterday a Shanghai professor pointed out the park on the Bund which once had the sign, "Chinese and dogs prohibited."

Air France stops at Rangoon and Karachi, then on to Paris. There I must try to give a conscientious picture of the Chinese economy.

September 23 — Paris

The Air France flight from just short of the Pacific on the Whampoa to just short of the Atlantic on the Seine must make for the longest night since the lights went out over Europe. You board just after dusk at 7:45 P.M.; if on schedule you dismount after dawn next morning at 7:30 A.M. That is 20 hours later. This morning we were an hour late in Paris for, because of an extra load, we had a "technical" stop in Athens to refuel. The extra load consisted of young Chinese in neat, black suits who nearly filled economy class. Tobin (who departed the plane in Karachi to go to Nairobi) identified them as workers on the way to Tanzania where the Chinese are building a railroad — and really doing the work. Alas for that explanation: Tobin left for Africa, and the Chinese continued on to Paris. Paris is as ever. The prospect of no ceremonial dinner is attractive.

September 24 — Paris

I've now managed to organize my view of the Chinese economy into a reasonably coherent whole. I've drawn primarily on our lectures at the University but also on numerous other discussions.

A description of an economic system turns on the answers — preferably the right ones — to a half-dozen basic questions. They are: What makes people work, which often, employment being unavailable or toil unpopular, they don't? And what things, in consequence, do people produce? And with what organization? And in response to what guidance or in accordance with what plan? And for whose benefit? And with how successful a result? There is the problem in all societies that the answers to these questions usually reflect the approved doctrine, not the reality. Thus the devout free enterpriser in the United States regularly pictures a freedom from government assistance, a level of competitive self-reliance, under which he could never survive. So it is also in a Communist country. The following deletes a certain amount of official doctrine. It is my view, not always that of our Chinese tutors, of the reality.

The first word must be said about the last question — that of the success of the economy. There can now be no serious doubt that China is devising a highly effective economic system. Development is from a very low level of per capita production, and that product is still low. With the liberation, decades of national and civil war, endemic pillage and public anarchy came to an end. Under almost any kind of economic system this would have led to economic gains. Law, order and honest government are very productive. But there is massive evidence of great continued movement — new housing, new industrial plants, new building at old plants, the impressive figures on the increase in local industrial and agricultural production and employment, the supply of basic staples in markets and shops, the people thronging through to buy them and the estimates of relative or percentage increases in production of agricultural and some industrial products. Without question we were taken to see and were told about the best. But in all travel one sees much that one is not shown, and Potemkin, whatever his skill, would have had more difficulty dealing with decently experienced economists.

Against this visual evidence is the nearly total absence of figures on absolute output, either of the economy as a whole or for individual industries or items. The figures are not published; the Chinese economists with whom we talked were forthcoming and helpful but did not appear to have them either. Frank Coe and Sol Adler, as I have mentioned, guess that the rate of expansion in Chinese industrial and agricultural output is now between 10 and 11 percent annually.[6] This does not seem to me implausible though it means a performance (always remembering the low point of departure) rivaling

[6] There is no Chinese figure for Gross National Product, i.e., total output including that of service enterprises and the government. This is considered a bourgeois concept.

that of Japan. But they do not know for sure, either. The Chinese economic system would not please most Americans or Europeans but it is not used by them. It does strike me as better adapted to its particular circumstance — more flexible, practical and dynamic and with a strikingly more successful protection of quality — than that of the socialist cum Communist states of the West. But let me get back to the questions.

People work for a variety of reasons. With us pecuniary incentives — principally the desire to make money — are greatly celebrated. But we also have people who march, as in the Marines or IBM, to the command of leaders, the desire for the good opinion of comrades or colleagues or in response to pride in the purposes of their outfit or organization. The Chinese have not rejected pecuniary incentives. As earlier noted, some 80 percent of the people are still associated with agriculture. The production team, the basic unit of the People's Commune, gets paid, less cost and taxes, what it earns. And members share in production in accordance with their hours of toil as modified by the point system. This is pecuniary reward in accordance with work performed. Similar incentive systems seem not to exist in larger-scale commerce or industry. But, we have seen, there is a modest graduation in accordance with skill, experience and responsibility.

But clearly the Chinese rely heavily — more heavily even than the other socialist economies — on organization. The economic system is a great battalion in which some lead, in which many march and in which there is much emphasis on the soldiers' sense of purpose. That the Chinese have a genius for organization seems to have been the revelation of an infinity of scholars. This capacity to enlist the energy of many for common purposes is everywhere in use. It involves unremitting exhortation — exhortation to work hard to build the nation, to ensure Chinese independence, to advance the revolution and, of course, to please Chairman Mao. Economic toil, and the resulting product, have been made identical with the highest national purpose. The emphasis on production as an end in itself now rather startles the American visitor. Evidently we have been getting economics into perspective in relation to other aspects of life. But it was not long ago that many Americans identified an increased National Product with all progress, and some still do.

To see the role of organization is to understand the otherwise (to me as to others) puzzling logic of the Great Proletarian Cultural Revolution. Organization is by its nature hierarchical — an organization is a built-in class system in which some command, many comply. The officer class has also a tendency to harden into a privileged and self-perpetuating caste which invites the next revolt. The Cultural Revolution attacked this tendency. Thus its emphasis on a reassociation of leadership with the masses and, at the more practical level, making the managerial, educational and other elites get out and do manual work themselves. There is a hint in the thought of Mao Tsetung that a periodic churning-up is necessary.

The Cultural Revolution, it may be noted, remains a major point of reference in all Chinese conversation. There was actual conflict in the industrial plants as well

121

as in the universities and elsewhere. (The countryside seems not to have been so much affected.) Industrial production has fully recovered. In factories, universities and even the secondary schools PLA representatives are still present, evidently as a stabilizing force. But in the industrial and commercial establishments, as well as from the economic reporting, one gets the impression of normal operations.

One thing is beyond doubt: The Chinese do work hard, effectively and intelligently for six days a week and without vacations. Vacations, as noted, are reserved for those who are separated by their work from their family. The impression of diligent effort — in town, countryside, construction sites, schools, public works — is overwhelming. Maybe there is a further explanation for this diligence. In the United States and Europe we greatly praise work. All good and honest people are held to rejoice in it. The work ethic and all that. This proposition we then deny by the attention we lavish in our economics and business practice on the means for making people expend energy. Maybe, in addition to all else, the Chinese, like the Japanese, really like to work. A disconcerting thought.

Work has a second dimension which is the opportunity; it doesn't matter how willing people are if there are no jobs available. In a heavily populated, agricultural country such as China or India there are three kinds of unemployment, namely (1) Ricardian unemployment, which means that because of the vast number of people in relation to land and capital there are many who cannot find jobs the product from which yields the equivalent of a living wage; (2) recurrent unemployment, which means that, given the nature of most agricultural operations, there are many dead hours in the day or days in the year when there is nothing to be done; and (3) disguised unemployment, which means that two or more people share tasks which could be done by one. The test of disguised unemployment, to repeat, is that, when the extra workers are withdrawn, production does not fall. A fourth kind of unemployment, the familiar Keynesian kind which plagues the Western economy, is not so serious. This unemployment is the result of a shortage of demand, and that tends to occur only when income and savings (which may not be invested or spent) are high.

The Chinese have tackled all their three kinds of unemployment. Recurrent and disguised unemployment are together the target of the industrial and handicraft enterprises on the commune. These use people who are seasonally idle or who cannot effectively be used or are not needed for crop production. They pay less than the urban industrial wage. But they use people who, otherwise, would be earning nothing. The opportunity cost of the labor is zero. No other country has attacked this problem of recurrent and disguised unemployment — the endemic waste of manpower in the Asian countryside — with the energy and imagination of the Chinese. One senses, also, that their effort still falls well short of solving the problem.

The attack on Ricardian unemployment is by a massive public employment program. The consequence has been sufficiently celebrated in the preceding pages — the meticulous cleaning and repair of streets, an attention to parks and gardens that approaches the English standard, high standards in other public housekeeping, extensive rehabilitation of public monuments, and the planting of the trees that I mentioned and that caused Barbara Tuchman to speak of the greening of China. Chinese economists now speak, perhaps a trifle disingenuously, of a labor shortage. It is, in part, the result of the lavish use of manpower for such work. The latter is doing wonders for both the countryside and the cities. It will be some time yet before a real labor shortage forces the Chinese to forgo street cleaning, park maintenance, flower planting and other practices now considered archaic in the more advanced economy.

Judging from the number of men (and fewer women) wearing the shapeless uniforms of the People's Liberation Army, military activity must also absorb a good deal of manpower. It is not a subject which a sensibly tactful visitor who also seeks information on more mundane matters should raise.

Coming to what the Chinese economy produces, the first choice, as everywhere, is between various things for present use and between such consumption and investment to increase output in the future. Let me begin with the last; it involves a most interesting point.

In the years following World War II the new Communist regimes of Eastern Europe, influenced more by ambition for the future than by present poverty, concentrated heavily on investment. The consumption of the current generation was sacrificed to the greater affluence of children and grandchildren. Rates of saving for investment were 30, 40, even 50 percent of product. The generation being so sacrificed to the future found the resulting sense of righteousness insufficient compensation for the current privation. Revolts or near revolts in Yugoslavia, East Germany, Poland, Hungary (of which there were also other causes) brought a sharp reversal of policy. What, partly by the accident of association, is called Stalinist economics came to an end. There was everywhere greater emphasis on consumer goods for current consumption.

Stalin (with Marx, Engels and Lenin) still survives in the Chinese Communist pantheon. His picture, deeply avuncular, is in most places of public ceremony. But the policy of planned deprivation associated with his name is strongly rejected. Investment in capital plant is high. Chinese experts assume a substantial military investment but concerning this also we did not ask. There is, however, much emphasis on the need for an immediate improvement in the standard of living. The first rule of Chinese planning (as put by one of the economists who briefed us) is "raising the living standards before accumulation." The priority that is accorded agriculture and light consumer industry as compared with heavy industry is much mentioned. Food, textiles and other elementary consumer products must be available in quantity sufficient for increased consumption before there can be allocation of product to investment. People must be persuaded that they are working for a stronger nation and a better future. But, as a wholly practical matter, they must see the bird in the hand.

Decision as to what consumer goods will be produced

(and which will have investment for future expansion) is facilitated in China by the low standard of living. There is an obtrusive quality about physical need. And so, in contrast with luxury products, the demand for goods that satisfy such need is relatively easy to predict. The first requirement, accordingly, is to fill the grain and clothing ration — rice or its cereal equivalent and cotton textiles are the two commodities that are rationed. Rationing, it may be noted, is all but universally regarded as a manifestation of scarcity. The Chinese speak with satisfaction about this or that product having been derationed. But it is also a useful device for securing to everyone an ample supply of an indispensable commodity at a stable price. There has been too much snobbish comment about the uniformity of Chinese clothing. General appearance is better, as noted, than on an American campus. But that is not the point. In a poor country an arrangement by which every person gets two sets of sound basic garments every year at low prices seems to me an exercise in the greatest good sense. The proper comparison of the comfortably clad Chinese is not with Americans or Europeans but with the huddled and half-clothed people of northern or upland India in the winter months.

Housing, health services and medicine are also produced in response to obvious physical requirements. Housing, especially in the cities, falls far short of physical need. The makeshift housing, so-called, is not on display but must be poor. Medicine and medical services, on the other hand, are major achievements. The cost of standard medicines is now about one-fifth the 1950 cost; the basic antibiotics, as I have mentioned, are available at nominal prices without prescription. I am prepared to believe that Greater Shanghai, with a population of around 12 million and its 424 hospitals, 44,000 beds and around 11,500 doctors (including the traditional practitioners), has a better medical service than New York. The average quality of practice is no doubt far higher in New York. But the chance of getting no care is also much higher. For the man who is dead because he cannot get to a doctor or get into a hospital or risk the resulting financial disaster, averages are very misleading. One gathers that health services in rural areas, especially the more remote ones, are much less good but also the object of much effort.

For other goods, production decisions are in response to consumer demand, reflected through a rough approximation to the ordinary price system. Prices of different products reflect different average costs with taxes and profit margins added. A premium (specifically unrelated to costs) is added for higher quality. This last, I judge to be very important in explaining the seemingly high quality of Chinese goods.

Interest is charged on borrowed capital. Currently the rate is 5.04 percent to industrial and commercial establishments, 4.56 percent to communes, 2.16 percent for basic construction and irrigation works. The People's Banks pay 3.24 percent on time deposits.[7] Interest rates, we were advised, are coming down. The prices once established, what people then buy determines what is produced. The prices of about 300 products come within the purview of

[7] The exceptional precision is caused by converting monthly rates used by the Chinese — one twelfth of the above — to a yearly basis.

the central government. The rest, called "small commodities," are set by state or local planning authorities although "sharp changes" must be reported to the central government. As in the West taxes on cigarettes (differing as between kinds of cigarettes), cosmetics and wines express social disapproval. The yield of the cosmetics tax cannot be large. Cigarette consumption is unapologetically high and, the taxes apart, still unresisted by the government. In consequence, and aided by an encouraging increase in air pollution, lung cancer is keeping pace with the general progress of civilization at least in the larger cities.

In agriculture the instrument of production is the People's Commune with, as in the case of the *kibbutzim*, its industrial sidearm. Elsewhere the basic instrument is the familiar and universal industrial firm. The People's Commune, to summarize, is a large, essentially administrative and policy organization. Membership ranges from 5000 or 6000 up to 10,000, and a few have 30,000 to 40,000. In units of this size obviously there can be no visible relationship between individual effort and result, and the same is true of the production brigade with a membership of around 1000. So, increasingly, the operating unit is the production team of 150 to 200 members. This deploys workers to their tasks; individual compensation is established according to the neo-socialist principle (as put by one of our discussants) of "Each does his best; each according to his work."

The tax on the commune remains fixed in absolute amount and thus declines with increasing output. It now

128

averages about 8 percent. After deduction of a percentage or two of the proceeds for management and 5 to 7 percent for welfare and capital accumulation, and the cost of fertilizer and other cash production expense, the receipts are divided between the teams in accordance with their production and by the teams, as noted, in accordance with the quantity and quality of each member's work.

On form, if there is a weakness in the Chinese economy, it should be here. Agriculture everywhere else in the world has yielded reluctantly and, more often than not, inefficiently to socialism. The production team seems still too large for the individual worker to see a close relationship between *his* work and reward. There must also, surely, be serious problems of administration. The mind boggles at the problem of getting good management for tens and hundreds of thousands of communes. But this is only a thought. For a serious judgment, one should see several hundred communes picked at random.

By U.S. or Japanese standards Chinese agriculture is grossly deficient in the use of commercial fertilizer — some Chinese leaders seem to take seriously the old peasant superstition that such fertilizer is damaging to the structure of the soil. Mechanization, even if not needed to conserve manpower, allows of better and more timely cultivation. Mechanization too must be slight. The extent of use of modern high-yielding hybrids is unclear. Progress, notwithstanding, has been substantial — grain production in 1971 was reported (one judges now reliably) at twice the low 1949 level, and cotton was up fourfold.

129

Given fertilizer, mechanization and the new hybrids, output could be very greatly increased. The Indian and Pakistani Punjab, which seems well ahead of China in this regard, has shown what is possible.

Except that there is no sales, merchandising, marketing or advertising staff — cadre is the word in Chinese — not much distinguishes the Chinese from the American or European industrial plant. For producing a given product, industrial plants are everywhere about the same. The terminology is different. Lee Iacocca, in a suitably large plant in Shanghai, would be the Principal Responsible Person; some more ceremonial figure, preferably Henry II, would be Chairman of the Revolutionary Committee. Leonard Woodcock would not at the moment be visible. Unions seem to have been a casualty of the Cultural Revolution. The factory would employ women indifferently along with men although men would still predominate in the executive and supervisory posts. The principal problem would still be getting out the product at low cost.

By the universally offered estimate, about 80 percent of the Chinese labor force is employed in, or in association with, agriculture but around 50 percent of the product, by value, comes from industry. And 90 percent of the revenue of the state is held to come from profits of, or taxes on, industrial and commercial enterprises or products. Incomes in agriculture are well below those in industry as Chinese economists concede — indeed stress. For this reason agricultural taxes are kept low. As a further corrective farm prices are kept relatively high and consumer food prices low, and the difference is made up with a subsidy from industrial profits and taxes. Agricultural income in communes in areas of high population but poor soil must be lower than in the better agricultural areas seen by the visitor. This would be the usual consequence of dividing less product among the same number of people.

As noted the Chinese appear to have developed a plain but remarkably efficient system for the distribution of consumer goods. The industrial establishments that we saw, a minuscule sample, seemed workmanlike, not over-manned and comparatively modern in their equipment. There can be few things, from a strict technological view-point, that the Chinese cannot — or do not — make. They may have been isolated in these last years but they have been studying lots of books, journals, models and products.

The flow of revenue from industrial profits and taxes has an admirable effect on Chinese public finance. The government has no external or internal debt — a loan from the Soviets negotiated at the time of the Korean war was paid off ahead of schedule in 1968. There is no income tax. The budget operates with a slight surplus. In our discussions in Peking information on Chinese finances was provided with great precision and competence by a member of the Institute of Economics of the Academy of Sciences.[8,9] One of the more engaging moments of the visit

[8] She noted that "The Chinese currency [is] one of the most stable in the world. In contrast with some capitalist countries, no borrowing, no inflation, no devaluation." Being, like all our hosts, impeccably polite she did not specify the capitalist country.
[9] The Institute of Economics is a sizable and prestigious research organi-zation still suffering, one member indicated, from some disorientation following the Cultural Revolution. As in Eastern Europe and the Soviet

was when James Tobin, who with Walter Heller was one of the men who made the New Economics legitimate under President Kennedy, undertook to explain in response to a question why it was often good for the United States to have a budget deficit and to increase its debt. He might have had it easier with Andrew Mellon.

In any other country (including the Soviet Union) the difference between urban and rural incomes that exists in China would set in motion a large movement of people to the cities, and in China it once did. This is not now happening. There is some recruitment of labor force in rural areas but, in the main, factories are staffed from the natural increase of population in the cities. The reason is straightforward: The Chinese are assigned to jobs, and they are required to remain where they are assigned. Though evidently enforced with some flexibility, this is not an arrangement that much appeals to the Western visitor. It does continue an antecedent practice by which people were held firmly in place by debt, poverty, ignorance or the condign punishment visited on deserters from armies of the state or the warlords. This was compulsion without saving security or reward.

Many details of Chinese planning are far from clear.

Union, work with a research institute appears to bring its members into much closer relationship with practical questions than does a position on a university economics faculty. Faculty members are more inclined, perhaps out of necessity, to substitute theory for fact, a circumstance not unknown with us. It might be added that if there is a dominant figure in Chinese economic planning, he is anonymous. Many will think that such anonymity for economists is a major contribution to culture and, given the high failure rate of economic ideas in all countries in recent times, sound personal strategy.

As described it begins with agriculture. A crop is projected which averages the past results of one bumper, two average and one poor harvest. From this come estimates as to the supply of food and industrial raw materials, notably cotton, jute and silk, that may be expected. The possible supply of cotton textiles and some other consumer goods can then be projected. The purchases of a population of modest and highly egalitarian income are predictable and wholly so for the rationed grain and cotton textiles. From the surplus of product over consumption needs comes an estimate as to what can be invested.

The resulting requirements for different commodities are distributed as targets to producers of consumer goods or, in combination with investment needs, to firms that produce capital goods or fill the production requirements of other firms. It seems possible that they are supplemented or filled out by orders directly from one firm to another. On this I am unclear. Aggregate income available for spending, an aspect of the conservative financial policy, is held down in relation to the expected supply of staple products. As a plausible result of this (and the highly egalitarian income distribution) queues, so familiar in front of the Soviet store, seem rare in China. People do not line up to buy what they do not have money to buy.[10]

This elementary planning framework involves a great many more problems than here implied. To ensure that the numerous production needs of one industry — spare

[10] My Harvard colleague Professor Dwight Perkins also stresses the firm control of wages including the absence (unlike in the Soviet Union) of competitive bidding for scarce kinds of manpower.

133

parts for textile machinery, tires for trucks — are available in adequate quantity from other industry and that there is balanced development (what the Chinese call, somewhat ambiguously, synthetic balance) between various branches of industry and agriculture is no slight task. Extensive calculation is involved; this is a task that, one assumes, would be facilitated notably by computers. Computer use, we were told, had been neglected in the past but it is now being energetically studied.

Some other details were also filled in. Where local products are produced for local markets, planning decisions are now being decentralized to provincial government. This decentralization with accompanying encouragement to local initiative in planning and development is greatly emphasized. Prices are fixed but where — as in the case of fruits and vegetables — supply can easily exceed or fall short of demand at the given price, there appears to be little hesitation in changing prices as needed "in a planned way." Industrial expansion is being encouraged in the cities of the interior, restrained on the coast. One economist said flatly that Shanghai was already "too big." Although the specification of definite production goals is thought important, there must be "leeway" in all planning for accommodation to particular need and circumstance. This flexibility is stressed. There is thought to be a place for industry of varying size: large, medium and small. The small local firm is obviously being thought of as one answer to the bureaucratic tendency of modern large-scale industry. Education, especially in the primary and secondary grades, has a major claim on resources, as do the medical services. Much emphasis is placed on the flow of recommendations up from the plants and workers: "Good plans are not made by a handful of people shut up in [a] room."

Earlier plans following the withdrawal of Soviet assistance and technicians stressed the self-sufficiency of China. The current five-year plan (which began in 1971) contemplates drawing on the best of foreign technology and accords an important role to foreign trade. The latter — now amounting to between 2 and 4 percent of agricultural and industrial output — will, one senses, remain small. Exports last year were divided almost equally as among industrial products, processed agricultural products and raw agricultural products, mainly rice. To the United States the Chinese foresee the export of "traditional" products including tea, silk, hog bristles and some foods. Prospective imports are industrial equipment, machines and aircraft. The communications satellite and the Boeings received particular mention. "Everything depends on the developing political situation."

The scale and character of the official planning establishment — national and provincial — is something of which we got no impression. One somehow has the feeling of a smaller and more flexible organization than the massive Soviet apparatus. But I would have difficulty adducing any evidence in support of that instinct.

As to whom the production is for, there is a quick and easy answer: It is for everyone in about the same amount. Somewhere in the recesses of the Chinese polity there may be a privileged Party and official hierarchy. Certainly it is the least ostentatious ruling class in history. So far as the visitor can see or is told, there is — for worker, technician, engineer, scientist, plant manager, local official, even, one suspects, table tennis player — a truly astonishing approach to equality of income. Older skilled workers, doctors and professors retain the higher incomes, rising to as much as Y300 or roughly U.S. $150 a month (though in basic purchasing power considerably more), that they had before the Cultural Revolution. But with age and retirement these higher incomes are being phased out. A younger generation from apprentice to plant manager is in the range from Y35 to a maximum of Y100 or Y150 a month, or roughly from $17 to $50 or at the very most $75. In agriculture, as noted, incomes are less. Since food and basic clothing are cheap, housing costs nominal and medical care mostly free, these are not starvation wages. The urban standard of living includes a bicycle, a watch and, in the few houses we saw, a sewing machine. In each excursion group thronging the parks and public monuments there is at least one camera. People reach places of work and recreation by public transportation that is cheap and looks efficient. Clearly there is very little difference between rich and poor.

One or two points seem worth additional emphasis. As compared with the Eastern European economies or that of the Soviet Union, the Chinese economy sustains a far lower standard of living. (There are far fewer automobiles than in India, and the shops are much plainer and less interesting. This, however, must be attributed not to a lower but a much more egalitarian living standard.) But along with the lower living standard goes a seemingly more effortless economy. One has the feeling, very simply, that the economy works better than in Russia or Poland — at least as I saw those countries a few years ago. Things in China give the impression of meshing; slighted workmanship, diminished quality are much less obvious. Something depends on the easy, affable and sensitive manners of the Chinese. One transfers his reaction to this to the society. Dissidents are brought firmly into line in China, but, one suspects, with great politeness. It is a firmly authoritarian society in which those in charge smile and say please. The leadership rebukes what is called "Commandism." And there is also the obvious willingness of the Chinese, given the opportunity, to work. But, for whatever reason, the Chinese economy appears to function very easily and well.

Thus the Chinese economic system. Ever since Lincoln Steffens returned from Russia to proclaim (to Bernard Baruch), "I have been over into the future and it works," travelers to the Communist countries have been reluctant to risk hard conclusions. When things went wrong, the skeptics remembered and rejoiced. One should not be craven. The Chinese economy isn't the American or European future. But it is the Chinese future. And let there be no doubt: For the Chinese it works.

September 25 — Long out of Orly

I was two days at the Ritz with no grievous sense of social guilt, no insuperable problem of cultural shock, wrote the foregoing summary of the Chinese economy, dined with Colette Modiano-Gustin who once wrote a very funny book about taking a French tourist party to China and Michelle Lapautre who sells my books in France. And I enriched Irwin Shaw, James Jones, Pat Lawford and any number of other people with my China memoirs. There was also a press conference and a money-raising dinner for George McGovern. The turnout for the dinner was adequate but not abundant. Now we are nearing Boston. It is a depressing prospect. For years I have been taking evasive action whenever I encountered a Harvard colleague whom I knew to have been traveling to some improbable place and who would wish to tell of his dreary adventures. I spot such people at the Faculty Club and sit at another table. I see them in the Yard and duck into Widener. If they invite us to dinner, I develop a sinus attack. They know what I've done. There is now no one, absolutely no one, who will want to listen to my China odyssey, which, unlike the annals of my friends, is really interesting. How sad! I should have foreseen that I would one day need an audience.

Index

WESTMAR COLLEGE LIBRARY